The Cosmic Mountain

The Cosmic Mountain

A Narrative Expedition Through the Bible

J. LEAVITT PEARL
and JOE D. SMITH

CASCADE *Books* • Eugene, Oregon

THE COSMIC MOUNTAIN
A Narrative Expedition Through the Bible

Copyright © 2025 J. Leavitt Pearl and Joe D. Smith. All rights reserved. Except for brief quotations in critical publications or reviews, no part of this book may be reproduced in any manner without prior written permission from the publisher. Write: Permissions, Wipf and Stock Publishers, 199 W. 8th Ave., Suite 3, Eugene, OR 97401.

Cascade Books
An Imprint of Wipf and Stock Publishers
199 W. 8th Ave., Suite 3
Eugene, OR 97401

www.wipfandstock.com

PAPERBACK ISBN: 979-8-3852-3376-2
HARDCOVER ISBN: 979-8-3852-3377-9
EBOOK ISBN: 979-8-3852-3378-6

Cataloguing-in-Publication data:

Names: Pearl, J. Leavitt [author]. | Smith, Joe D. [author].

Title: The cosmic mountain : a narrative expedition through the Bible / by J. Leavitt and Joe D. Smith.

Description: Eugene, OR: Cascade Books, 2025 | Includes bibliographical references and index.

Identifiers: ISBN 979-8-3852-3376-2 (paperback) | ISBN 979-8-3852-3377-9 (hardcover) | ISBN 979-8-3852-3378-6 (ebook)

Subjects: LCSH: Mountains—Religious aspects. | Mountains in the Bible. | Bible—Theology.

Classification: BL447 L43 2025 (paperback) | BL447 (ebook)

VERSION NUMBER 092325

Scripture quotations are taken from the New Revised Standard Version Updated Edition. Copyright © 2021 National Council of Churches of Christ in the United States of America. Used by permission. All rights reserved worldwide.

For First United Methodist Church of Pittsburgh
and Baldwin Community United Methodist Church

They will not hurt or destroy
on all my holy mountain,
for the earth will be full of the knowledge of the LORD
as the waters cover the sea.

—Isaiah 11:9

Contents

Acknowledgements | IX
Introduction | XI

   1 Eden: The Mountain of Co-Creation | 1

   2 Hermon: The Mountain of Cosmic Revolt | 12

   3 Moriah: The Mountain of Sacrifice | 24

   4 Sinai: The Mountain of Covenant | 33

   5 Zion: The Mountain of Divine Dwelling | 45

   6 Horeb: The Mountain of Sacred Silence | 56

   7 Tabor: The Mountain of Unveiling | 67

   8 Golgotha: The Mountain of Death | 76

   9 Olivet: The Mountain of Absence | 86

  10 The New Eden: The Mountain of Re-Creation | 99

Study Guide | 110
Bibliography | 131
Ancient Documents Index | 135

Acknowledgements

A CO-AUTHORED BOOK IS a dance—a unique experience of persuasion, compromise, and improvisation. But the truth is no book is written alone. It was Bogdan Bucur who, in a doctoral seminar at Duquesne University, first introduced us both to the idea of cosmic mountains. But more importantly, he managed to reignite a love for the Bible in a couple of jaded young systematic theology graduate students who had hardly opened one in years. We each developed these ideas in our own classrooms and church small groups and in conversations with friends, colleagues, parishioners, and students—far too many to name but all of whom gave this book its shape and texture.

A number of friends and colleagues read all or part of the manuscript and offered invaluable feedback: Tina Whitehead, Steven Tuell, Bogdan Bucur, Danielle Shroyer, Gwendolen Jackson, Drew Dunbar, RoBear Wilson, and Harley Baldwin White-Wiedow. The book is clearer and richer for their guidance. Where it retains mistakes is likely where we failed to heed it. We appreciate the wisdom and support of our editor Robin Parry and the team at Wipf and Stock, who saw the manuscript to completion. We certainly would not have made it through the long and sometimes arduous process of writing this book if not for the patience, love, and encouragement of our families and friends. Finally, we want to express our deep gratitude to First United Methodist Church of Pittsburgh and Baldwin Community United Methodist Church, the communities who inspired this work and to whom, in return, it is our gift.

Introduction

TWO CHERUBIM—MENACING, DIVINE WARRIOR figures—stand guard at the entrance to Eden, wielding incandescent swords. The place where the heavens and the earth once converged, from which life-giving divine energy once flowed to the world, has been abandoned and is overgrown—wild and waste. Human beings, forged as idols and avatars of the Creator and given wide latitude in the ministration of creation, have chosen instead the destructive spirit of Babylon, the way of coercive power.

The Bible is the epic tale of a god's quest to overcome this alienation, to partner with a people to restore creation. The path is winding and uncertain, and obstacles—both cosmic and mundane—stand in the way. But the stakes are nothing less than the fate of creation itself.

WHY THIS BOOK?

This is the story that I (Joe) try to imprint in different ways upon the hearts and minds of my university students and the parishioners of the small, progressive United Methodist Church where I serve as a director of spiritual formation. I remember a sermon I gave early in my tenure there from the New Testament book of Hebrews. Hebrews is written to a community that had suffered persecution for their faith in Jesus—possibly under the Emperor Nero. They were dejected and afraid.[1] Many were considering giving up on their faith. The author wants to remind her dispirited audience that as bad as things look, they can put their hope in something they cannot see. To make the case, the writer paints with dramatic prose a picture of two mountain peaks: "You have not come to something that can be touched," she writes, "a blazing fire, and darkness, and gloom, and a tempest, and the

---

1. Some authors have suggested that the author of Hebrews was Priscilla. See, e.g., Hoppin, *Priscilla's Letter*.

sound of a trumpet, and a voice whose words made the hearers beg that not another word be spoken to them" (Heb 12:18–19).

I explained that the place the author of Hebrews is describing here is Mount Sinai (though it is unnamed in the text). She's referring to a story found in Exodus chapters 19–24. While everyone else present was held back by a blazing fire and a whirring tempest, Moses scaled the mountain and disappeared into a thick dark cloud. He emerged forty days later having received the law and the blueprint for the tabernacle.

But the author of Hebrews tells their audience they have not come to this mountain, where the divine presence is so thick and overwhelming that most people cannot even approach it. Instead, she assures them that they stand upon an unseen heavenly mountain, imperceptible to ordinary consciousness: "You have come to Mount Zion and to the city of the living God, the heavenly Jerusalem, and to innumerable angels in festal gathering, and to the assembly of the firstborn who are enrolled in heaven, and to God the judge of all" (Heb 12:22–23).

I explained that both of these—Mount Sinai and Mount Zion—are biblical examples of the ancient notion of a cosmic mountain, a place of unique divine presence, where the heavens and the earth touch. I walked my audience through other cosmic mountain images in the Bible: Mount Moriah, Mount Tabor, and the Mount of Olives. I showed how the author of Hebrews drew all these images together to create a dynamic tension in the book.

After church, Heather came up to talk to me. She had been the lector that morning—the person responsible for reading the Scripture text aloud before it is expounded upon in the sermon. She was frustrated with herself because, even though she had read the Hebrews text several times in preparation for the service, she had failed to see many of the things that I drew out. She wanted to know how she could learn to read the Bible the way I had in my sermon. Heather is intelligent and highly educated, so I knew the issue wasn't with her. The problem is the way we are accustomed to reading the Bible in church. We read little bite-sized chunks disconnected from their context. I told Heather that she just needed to get a sense of the overarching narrative of the Bible. Then all the pieces would fall into place. She thanked me and I walked away feeling pretty good about myself.

But on the drive home, I realized how stupid it was of me to have left her with that advice. *Just get a sense of the overarching narrative of the Bible.* Great! How in the world was she supposed to do that? It's not that it was bad advice, exactly. Learning the grand story of the Bible *is* the best way to make sense of the fragments we hear in church every week. But finding the narrative thread that runs through so bewildering a collection of texts as the Bible isn't easy to do.

Later that evening, I called Heather to apologize for my glib and useless advice, which she accepted graciously. I told her that I would find a resource to help her understand the large-scale story of the Bible. I was sure that once she had that story firmly fixed in her mind then all of the smaller episodes would start to make sense. As soon as we finished talking, I sat down at my desk and went to work searching for a book that would help Heather see the big picture. But my efforts led only to frustration.

I found lots of accessible and engaging books about what the Bible is and how to read it. Rob Bell's *What Is the Bible?* (HarperOne, 2017), Rachel Held Evans' *Inspired* (Nelson, 2018), and Peter Enns' *How the Bible Actually Works* (HarperOne, 2019) stand out as excellent recent examples. What I didn't find was any book written from a progressive Christian perspective that actually does a narrative reading of the Bible. I was at a loss for what to recommend to Heather. I needed some help.

I called my friend, Justin Leavitt Pearl, a fellow theology professor who at the time was also serving as an education director at a United Methodist Church. We decided to meet up for a drink at a bar on the south side of Pittsburgh. I told him about my sermon and Heather's question. I lamented that I couldn't find any resources to help her or the other members of my church get a handle on the narrative arc of the Bible. I knew that Justin was just as interested as I was in a narrative reading of the Bible because we had collaborated often on teaching introductory Bible courses in our university classrooms. I was sure he could help me find something. Imagine my disappointment when Justin told me that he too had been searching in vain for an easy way to help his church members understand the overarching story of the Bible. At that moment, it became clear what we needed to do. We ordered another round and we outlined this book on a cocktail napkin.

THE BIBLES I HAVE READ

My conversation with Heather got me thinking about how I learned to read the Bible the way I do. I grew up in church, so every Sunday morning of my formative years I sat in a plastic chair twisting colorful pipe cleaners around popsicle sticks. When craft time was over, my peers and I would get a snack

Introduction

of crackers or cookies and our teacher would read us a Bible story—usually one featuring animals, like Noah's Ark or Jonah and the Whale. Then she would explain to us the "moral" of the story. Invariably it was that Jesus wanted us to share our toys, listen to our parents, or not pinch our siblings. So, like many people with a background similar to mine, the first Bible I read was something rather like Aesop's *Fables*: short, self-contained animal stories written to give clear, universally applicable moral guidance.

As I got older my Bible reading grew with me. By way of sticker charts and elaborate reward systems, my Sunday school teachers encouraged me to memorize important Bible verses word-for-word in the King James Version. Now, instead of learning the morals of the Bible's animal stories, we would practice our memorization with games that we—borrowing another image from the book of Hebrews—called "sword drills." Occasionally, we would even put our mnemonic prowess to the test by competing against the youth of other churches to win the coveted Bible Bowl trophy. Having matured beyond the need for our teachers to tell us the moral of a Bible story, we were encouraged to discover for ourselves how the verses we had memorized applied to our lives. Most of them, it seemed to me, addressed my teenage angst and insecurities. The Bible had morphed from a book of fables into a calendar with inspirational quotes on every page.

In college, I decided to study theology, a field that includes, among other things, the academic study of the Bible and other holy books and their reception history. After college, I went on to pursue graduate degrees in theology, concentrating on the New Testament and early Christianity. There I learned to do what scholars call a historical-critical reading of the Bible. The idea of historical-critical biblical scholarship is that every text is written to meet some specific need of a community. In some instances, there may be a real historical event underlying a biblical story, however different it may have been from its interpretation and depiction in the text. But even then, the story of that event is told in such a way as to deliver a specific message to a particular group of people living at the time and in the place the text was written. The role of the historical-critical scholar is to deconstruct the text and reconstruct the social and cultural particularities, religious beliefs and practices, and political persuasions of the author or editors of the text and of their community. As I looked back with an air of condescension on the Bibles I used to read—the book of fables and the inspirational quotes calendar—the Bible transfigured yet again. This time it had become a puzzle to be solved.

Introduction

Now I live in two worlds at once. In my classes at Duquesne University, I teach my students the same historical-critical method I learned in graduate school. Even though Duquesne is a Roman Catholic institution, my students come from diverse religious backgrounds. And though I teach the Bible and other religious texts, I do not assume any religious commitment on the part of my students. There is a historical puzzle behind these texts and I give my students the tools to solve it. But I also work in a church. Unlike my university classrooms, my church is a Christ-centered community, where faith is woven into every dimension of our lives. Even here, I sometimes find that historical-critical tools help to illuminate certain aspects of a passage of Scripture that might otherwise be obscure. But mostly I guide folks through a meditative style of Bible reading called *lectio divina*, or "sacred reading."

Developed by Benedictine monks in the sixth century CE, *lectio divina* is not principally concerned with the historical or literary context of a passage, or with its function in the narrative structure of the biblical canon. Rather, one reads to commune with the divine through the text. So the reading is slow—meandering, even—and the meaning discovered in the text is unique to each reader and different with each reading. In that sense, the Bible becomes something of a Rorschach test: readers look deeply into the images of the Bible and find there a mirror reflecting, however dimly, the deepest longings of their own soul.

I have read many Bibles in my life: Bibles that look like a book of fables, an inspirational quotes calendar, a puzzle, and a Rorschach test. But none of these images quite capture how we will read the Bible in this book. Rather, I'd like to propose a fifth metaphor—the *epic novel*. This book offers a narrative reading of the story that runs in, through, and underneath the Jewish and Christian Scriptures. Like *The Odyssey*, *Lord of the Rings*, or *Game of Thrones*, the Bible is a grand narrative spread across centuries. It incorporates countless characters, unexpected plot developments, and complex literary allusions. This is a deeply human story—full of sex and murder, passion and regret, love and betrayal. But through all of the twists and turns, there remains a core narrative driving the text forward. In this book, we want to show you how to discover this narrative within the Bible.

Introduction

A NARRATIVE READING OF THE BIBLE

Historically speaking, it is rather strange that we have this Bible sitting on our coffee table right now. The Bible is an exceedingly rare kind of book. It's not exactly a book at all. It's hard to remember this because we bind it together in a single cover, so that it looks like a book. But the Bible is a library. It includes mythology, history books, regulatory law, census data, poetry, song lyrics, political punditry, reports of mystical visions, short stories, biographies, sermons, letters, and more. These were written over about a thousand years, in at least three different languages, by dozens of people who had no notion what they were writing would be gathered into a collection like this, let alone that many would one day consider it Holy Writ. But they were collected by other people and edited and arranged into something like a scrapbook that would tell the story of a people and the god they wrestle with. Of course, every culture has its mythologies and its philosophers. But not many thought to gather all these important writings into one place. Judaism and Christianity are an exception in this regard. Jews collected their mythologies, founding stories, laws, and social prophets into a canon (an official collection of writing for legal or religious use), which they call the Tanakh. Early Christians, most of whom in the earliest days of the movement were Jews, expanded the canon (which Christians later called the Old Testament), thereby giving their own fresh interpretation to it. The early Christian expansion of these Scriptures is called the New Testament.

Having grown so accustomed to seeing the Bible bound together as a single book, it is hard to see how strange this idea of canonization is. It would be like if we bound Stephen Hawking's *A Brief History of Time*, the libretto of *Hamilton*, The United States Constitution, the lyrics from Abbey Road, the speeches of Martin Luther King, Jr. and Malcolm X, a handful of Noam Chomsky's personal letters, and Al Gore's *An Inconvenient Truth* all in a single paperback published by Random House. Behind this incredible impulse to canonize lies the conviction that all of the Bible's disparate writings weave together into one coherent tapestry. The Bible is an unfolding drama that tells the story of the Creator's adventures in trying to renew and dwell within creation.

This narrative reading of the Bible is different from any of the other ways that I read the Bible throughout my life. That's not to say that a narrative reading is the "right" way to read the Bible, or even that it's better than other ways I have read the Bible. It's just different. Many of the other ways of reading the Bible still have their place in my life. I still use the historical-critical method in my university classroom and *lectio divina* is still an important practice for me in devotional settings like the church. The Bible is multifaceted, like a well-cut diamond. It reflects light differently when you look at it from different angles. So in this book, for instance, we won't suggest that you "apply the Bible to your life," as I was encouraged to do when I was reading the Bible like a book of fables or a calendar with inspirational quotes. Instead, we will try to paint a picture of the biblical world so big and so strange that you can get lost in it. Rather than extracting meaning out from the Bible, which you can apply to your already well-defined life, we hope that you will find your life *in* the biblical narrative.

Further, the narrative reading of the Bible presented in this book is not a devotional reading like the *lectio divina* I teach at church. To be sure, there is a pious history that underlies the collection of all the disparate writings that make up the Bible into a canon. The Jews who formed the Tanakh did so because they believed that these writings, edited and arranged in the right way, would tell the story of their people and their god. The Christians who arranged these same Scriptures into what they called the Old Testament, and expanded it with their own writings in the New Testament, did so because they believed that the story of Israel's god took on a new shape in the life of Jesus of Nazareth and in the community of his followers. But you don't have to be a Jew or a Christian, or even believe in a god, to enjoy or find meaning in this story. For the Bible, like all good stories, is the human story. It is a story of love and tragedy, hope and despair. It invites us into the deep questions of life: Why are we here? Who is in charge? Why do we feel such a deep ache? What are we supposed to do? Is everything going to be okay?

Finally, reading narratively also entails suspending some historical judgments. The historical-critical method I learned in graduate school is often described as "demythologizing" the Bible—clearing the mythological elements of the biblical narratives in an effort to excavate any real historical events that underlie those stories and to understand the real historical communities for which they were written.[2] We hope to re-mythologize the

---

2. This term was coined by Rudolf Bultmann, one of the greatest New Testament scholars of the twentieth century. Bultmann seems to have meant by the term that the New Testament should be read as myth in order to determine where the texts have "a still deeper meaning which is contained under the cover of mythology." Bultmann, *Jesus Christ and Mythology*, 18.

Bible. We are trying, not to unearth its historical antecedents, but to bring to life its exotic and fantastical narrative world.

1

Eden
The Mountain of Co-Creation

In the sixth Book of the *Odyssey*, the goddess Athena ascends to the top of Mount Olympus. This peak, according to Homer, is "The unmoving abode of the gods, unshaken by winds, never soaked by rain, and where the snow never drifts, but the brilliant sky stretches cloudless away, and brightness streams through the air. There, . . . the gods are happy all the world's days."[1] Mount Olympus is a paradigmatic example of a "cosmic mountain," a site of unique divine presence.

With examples as far flung as Mount Fuji, the holiest site in the indigenous Japanese Shinto religion; Machu Picchu, the site of the famous ancient Incan citadel in southern Peru; and Matȟó Paha (or Bear Butte) in South Dakota, sacred to the Sioux and Cheyenne peoples; cosmic mountains are understood by those who hold them sacred as the center of the universe. They are the cradle of creation, the place from which all things come into being.

Gods reign from atop cosmic mountains. Among the Chagga people of Tanzania, Mount Kilimanjaro is home to the god Ruwa. Mount Kailash in Tibet is the abode of the Hindu deities Shiva and Parvati. Cosmic mountains are, thus, the place where humans encounter the divine—what Homer calls the "heavenly threshold."[2] This is why Mount Meru, the five-peaked

---

1. Homer, *Odyssey*, 6.43–47.
2. Homer, *Iliad*, 1.590.

cosmic mountain of many traditions originating in southeast Asia, provides the sacred blueprint for many Hindu, Jain, and Buddhist temples.

Peculiarly, cosmic mountains are also (usually) real mountains. Meru almost certainly had, at one time, a specific geographical referent among the Pamir Mountains of South and Central Asia, though its precise location is no longer known. Mount Olympus is a national park in Eastern Greece. You can vacation there today. You can climb Mount Olympus in a weekend, swim at its waterfalls, and have a nice picnic. Such is the paradox of the cosmic mountain. It is at once sacred and mundane, terrestrial and divine. The cosmic mountain is the place where the heavens and the earth overlap.

While cosmic mountain ideology is certainly prevalent in "pagan" texts like the *Iliad* and the *Odyssey*, it is no less present in the worldviews of the biblical authors.[3] For example, in the Bible, Mount Zion is the abode of the god of Israel. But this mount (really it's more of a hill) sits at the center of modern-day Jerusalem. People live and work across Mount Zion. You can pick up a nice scarf or some great falafel there.

It was at Mount Zion that Nebuchadnezzar II, the ruthless king of the Neo-Babylonian Empire, culminated his brutal twenty-four-month siege against the kingdom of Judah in 588 BCE. Nebuchadnezzar's empire-building campaign across the ancient Near East came on the heels of a similar advance by the Assyrian Empire, which had destroyed Judah's northern neighbor, Israel, only a few years earlier. When they finally marched on the capital, Nebuchadnezzar's army executed the royal family in front of the Jewish king Zedekiah before gouging out his eyes—the death of his family would be the last thing he ever saw. They plundered and then razed the holy temple to the ground. Citizens who survived the assault were led on a crippling march to the city of Babylon, where they would live under the heel of a foreign king, in exile from their homeland. It was during this exile that the Jews began to compile what came to be known as the Torah, or the teachings—the first five books of what we now know as the Tanakh or the Christian Old Testament.

A COSMIC CREATION POEM

Our story begins with a poem about an unnamed god creating the heavens and the earth, fashioning them out of the chaos and darkness that covers

---

3. See Levenson, *Sinai and Zion*; Clifford, *Cosmic Mountain*; Morales, *Tabernacle Pre-figured*.

the face of the deep. Before there is anything—before there is land or plants, stars or sky, creeping crawlers or the great creatures of the seas—there are only dark, chaotic waters. In the ancient Hebrew imagination, the chaotic waters are an inhospitable place where nothing can flourish. But this god passes over the waters like a gentle breeze and begins to speak.

On the first day, the god says, "Let there be light," and there is light. The god sees that the light is good and separates the light from the darkness. The former is named "day," the latter "night." These terms mark out places where heavenly bodies—like the sun, moon, and stars—can dwell. There is evening and morning on the first day.

This first act of creation sets a model for the rest of the poem. Hebrew poetry rhymes, but not with syllables like English poetry; it rhymes with concepts. This poem, for instance, has a cyclical structure: First, the god says, "let there be . . ." and something is. Then, They[4] identify that something as "good." Finally, They divide the something in half and name the two halves. And there is evening and there is morning.

And so, on the second day, the god separates the water above from the water below. What water above?, you might ask. To understand this, you have to get into the mindset of ancient cosmology. Imagine you're an ancient person without the benefit of telescopes, pictures from space, or modern physics textbooks. If you walk outside and look around, it isn't immediately obvious that you are on a globe. It looks like you're on a flat plane under a large dome. This is exactly what the authors of this creation poem thought. But they also noticed something strange. Water sometimes falls down out of the sky. Whatever the dome above you is, apparently it leaks. Where is it leaking from? Well, there must be water up there. Similarly, if you start digging down into the earth, you will eventually find water. Indeed, if you want safe drinking water in a world before purification systems, digging a well is probably your best bet. Thus, they logically concluded, there is water below, too. In fact, there seems to be water everywhere. No matter what direction you walk in, you will eventually come to an ocean.

---

4. We believe that the Divine Mystery transcends and includes the entire spectrum of gender identity and expression. Unfortunately, English pronouns traditionally have not. But in recent years, trans and non-binary folks have gifted the anglophone world with the singular use of they/them/their pronouns for referring to people who do not fit comfortably into our tired binary boxes. We will refer to the god of Scripture, too, with capitalized pronouns They/Them/Their. This usage at once affirms the gender-expansive character of the Divine Mystery (Gen 1:27) and gives a subtle nod to the interplay between unity and plurality in the Christian doctrine of the Trinity.

Judging this data, the ancient Hebrews came to the straightforward conclusion that they were entirely surrounded by water. Water above, water below. In this cosmology, the entire cosmos is carved out of the chaotic deep like a giant air bubble floating in the vast, seething ocean without surface.

On the third day, the god separates the waters below into rivers, lakes, and oceans to expose dry land. This land is called "earth." It is good. And there is evening and there is morning on the third day.

If the repetition—"let there be . . . ," "it is good," separation, naming, evening and morning—is the rhythm of the poem, then its harmony is found in the parallelism *between* the days. If you look closely, you might notice a pattern. During the first three days, the god builds spaces: day and night, sky and sea, and dry land. Having created these diverse spaces, this god spends the next three days filling these spaces with creatures designed to flourish in each domain. On day four, the god places lights in the spaces of day and night: "a greater light [the sun] to rule the day and the lesser light [the moon] to rule the night" (1:16), as well as stars. On day five, the god says, "Let the waters bring forth swarms of living creatures . . . sea monsters and every living creature" and "every winged bird" (1:20–21), to fill the spaces of sea and sky respectively. On day six, "every creeping thing that creepeth" fills the dry earth created on day three (1:26, KJV). The poem culminates with the creation of humankind "in the image" (1:27) of the god. It is all very good.

A SECOND CREATION MYTH

This poem isn't the only account of creation in the biblical texts. Alternate stories, songs, and poems about creation can be found in Psalm 8 and 104, Job 38, Proverbs 8, and John 1, to name a few. The Bible is littered with accounts of creation. And, unfortunately for the literalist, these accounts seldom agree. Indeed, the very next chapter of Genesis gives a completely independent creation myth—an older story, whose vocabulary and style make clear that it was written by a different author. But the editors and compilers of the Torah were perfectly happy to place this alternate myth side-by-side with the more recent poem.

The second creation account begins not with chaotic waters, but an inhospitable desert—dry cracked ground from which no life has ever, or could ever, emerge. For, we are told, YHWH (here, we finally get the name of the unnamed god),[5] "had not caused it to rain upon the earth, and there was no one to till the ground" (Gen 2:5). And so, YHWH takes these two problems in turn. First, They draw a stream out of the ground to water the land. What do you get when you mix water with the dirt of an arid desert? Clay. YHWH digs up some of the clay and begins to mold a statue. They breathe into the statue and transform it into the first living, breathing human being—Adam, whose name is etymologically related to the word for "earth" or "dirt."

This scene might seem a little strange. But it would have been perfectly clear to the original audience of this text. This process directly mimics an idol-making practice common throughout the ancient Near East. Artisans would construct statues of gods from wood, metal, or clay. Then, in a ceremony referred to as "the opening of the mouth," they would ritually breathe into the statues, marking the moment when they mystically became living, breathing gods.[6] This is why the Hebrew prophets frequently mocked the idols of Canaanite religions, saying they have no breath in them.

> What use is an idol
>   once its maker has shaped it—
>   a cast image, a teacher of lies?
> For its maker trusts in what has been made,
>   though the product is only an idol that cannot speak!
> Alas for you who say to the wood, "Wake up!"
>   to silent stone, "Rouse yourself!"
>   Can it teach?

---

5. Throughout this book, we refer to the creator-god of Israel by the proper name most commonly used in the Hebrew Bible, YHWH. Following Jewish custom—in which this name is not pronounced—we invite you to read this name as "*Hashem*" (literally, "the Name"). English translations of the Bible pay homage to this custom by rendering the divine name "the LORD" in all capital letters. Where we quote directly from the Bible, we have left this translation intact.

We hope that our using the divine name will help readers be mindful of the fact that we are talking, not about an abstract concept or entity called "God," but about a specific, *named* deity. At the same time, we recognize that in other respects this convention will muddy the waters. In the creation poem of Genesis 1, for instance, the creator isn't named YHWH, but *Elohim. Elohim*—and its singular form, *El*—is both a proper name and as close a Hebrew equivalent as you will find to the English word "god." This discrepancy likely reflects the fact that Judaism was born out of an ancient culture in which many gods and goddesses were worshiped. By the time the Hebrew Bible was collected into its current form, YHWH and *El/Elohim* had effectively blended into a single deity, though residue of the earlier traditions remains in the texts. On that, see Smith, *Early History of God*.

6. McDowell, *Image of God in the Garden of Eden*.

> See, it is gold and silver plated,
>> and there is no breath in it at all. (Hab 2:18–19)

The incredible claim that the Genesis 2 narrative proposes, then, is this: in creating humans, *YHWH made an idol of Themselves.* In fact, the word *tselem*, used in the Genesis 1 poem to say that humans are created in YHWH's "image," is used elsewhere in the Tanakh as a synonym for idols. For example, a priest named Jehoiada—after he had staged a coup against the Baal-worshiping Queen Athaliah[7]—took "all the people of the land [and] went to the house of Baal and tore it down; his altars and his images (*tsĕlāmîm*) they broke in pieces" (2 Kgs 11:18). At the same time, the injunction against making graven images in the ten commandments echoes the language of Genesis 1: "You shall not make for yourself an idol, whether in the form of anything that is in heaven above or that is on the earth beneath or that is in the water under the earth" (Exod 20:4). These parallelisms suggest that the reason the Hebrew people were told not to make idols of YHWH is that all the necessary idols of YHWH have already been created. And you're one of them!

YHWH plants a garden in this land—which we now learn is called Eden—and places the first human there. Trees and plants of all sorts, "every tree that is pleasant to the sight and good for food" (Gen 2:9) bursts forth from the ground. In the middle of the garden stands the tree of life. The life-giving power of YHWH radiates from this tree, as four rivers flow from the center of the garden.

Adam works the soil of the garden. But he is understandably lonely. And so YHWH decides to make him a partner. First, YHWH creates the animals but none are suitable partners for Adam. So, YHWH places Adam into a deep sleep and performs a bit of late-night improvised surgery—removing a rib from his side and using it to craft a partner for him. She is named Eve, which means "life." These two tend the land together as equals—for the violence of gendered hierarchy has not yet entered the world.

---

7. Athaliah—the only queen regent in Judah/Israel's history—is not particularly well regarded in the Bible, both because of the brutality with which she ascended to the throne and because she continued to support the cult of Baal worship begun by her father, King Ahab. Nevertheless, she briefly succeeded in reuniting the two kingdoms. See 2 Kgs 11 and 2 Chr 22:10—23:21.

NOTHING THAT EVER WAS

Both the poetic and the narrative creation accounts are mythological. When we say that the opening chapters of Genesis are myths, we don't mean that they're untrue. To say that a story is myth isn't the same thing as saying it is false. What we do mean, in part, is that these stories don't equate truth with historical and scientific factuality. That equation is an entirely modern way of thinking. The poets who composed these creation myths could not be less interested in a literal or scientific description of the world and its early history. They had a different project—a poetic and artistic project to uncover another sort of truth. Myths explore the deep, existential truths about divinity, humanity, and the world. By employing often fantastical images, stories, and symbols, myths engage the imagination to ask the deep questions: Why are we here? What does it mean to be human? What is the divine like? Is the world ultimately good? As one ancient author said: *myth describes nothing that ever was, but what always is.*[8]

In this sense, it doesn't really matter that these two creation texts don't exactly line up in their descriptive details. The editors and compilers weren't interested in smoothing them into a seamless monotony. Instead, these two stories stand together in their wild diversity and difference. Two unique images of creation. Two different, beautiful accounts of the nature and destiny of humanity and the meaning of the universe.

Despite their diversity in the poetic and symbolic register, however, the meaning of these two texts is surprisingly consistent. Here's one example of how the two creation myths differ in detail but align in meaning. Genesis 1 begins with deep, dark waters, while Genesis 2 starts with the completely inverted image of an arid desert.

> Darkness covered the face of the deep, while a wind from God swept over the face of the waters. (Gen 1:2)

> No plant of the field was yet in the earth and no vegetation of the field had yet sprung up—for the LORD God had not caused it to rain upon the earth, and there was no one to till the ground. (Gen 2:4b–5)

These images are opposites but their mythic function is the same. Both dark waters and arid deserts are symbols of chaotic inhospitality, places where life cannot flourish. Whether you drown in an ocean or dehydrate

---

8. This insight is traditionally ascribed to Sallustius, a fourth-century Roman philosopher.

in a desert, you're dead all the same. The symbolism here is pointing to the goodness of YHWH's creation, which rescues us from the dusty desert or the watery depths. In this way of thinking, the world of creation is just as much an island in a stormy sea as an oasis in a harsh desert. It is a place designed for life to flourish. This is a pretty bold claim to be made by a bunch of slaves living in exile. But this isn't all that these narratives are trying to communicate. As you sort through all the little details, something remarkable emerges.

COSMIC TEMPLE-MOUNTAIN

In Genesis 1, the first mythic poem, the author appears to be narrating a building project. YHWH builds the rooms of a cosmic house—day and night, sea and sky, and dry land—and then furnishes these rooms in the order in which they were built. This construction moves according to a ritualized, cyclical rhythm—"there was evening, and there was morning."

Moreover, YHWH doesn't retain exclusive control over the creative process. Everything in the building takes part in the act of creation. Creation is itself a co-creator. The greater and lesser lights don't just hang there in the sky like lightbulbs. They are tasked with ruling over the day and night (1:16), just as human beings are given dominion over the lower regions of sea, air, and earth (1:28). YHWH doesn't even seem to create plant and animal life, as such. Rather, the land is commanded to "put forth vegetation" from itself (1:11). This isn't too surprising—we're used to seeing plants just burst forth from the ground. But YHWH also commands the waters of the sea to bring forth swarms of living creatures and the earth to bring forth the creeping things (1:20, 24). Even the animals are told to "be fruitful and multiply" and to "fill the earth" (1:22, 28), thereby continuing the ongoing work of creation. Creation isn't a one-person show; it's a cooperative project in which YHWH shares power, vulnerably handing the reins (and the reign) to creation itself. As an ancient rabbi once put it: "from the first day of creation the Holy One, blessed be He, longed to enter into partnership with the terrestrial world."[9]

A large building. Rhythmic cycles. Many hands working together to increase divine glory. To the modern reader, that might not sound like anything in particular, but to the ancient readers and hearers of this poem, the

---

9. *B'reishit Rabbah* 3.9. Or, as the Jewish Talmud similarly put it: we are all, each one of us, "a partner in the work of creation." *b. Shabbat* 119b.

meaning would have been unmistakable: Genesis 1 is about the building of a temple. In other words, *all of creation is a temple.*

According to the ancient conception, the temple is where the divine dwells. It's not for nothing that the Tanakh will later name the temple the "house of God." By housing the divine glory, the temple is the center of all life, energy, and meaning. And from the temple, that life-giving divine energy flows out to the rest of the world.

Let's rewind for a second. Remember that, at the time that this poem is being compiled, the people of Judah are exiled in Babylon. Their king is blinded and chained. His heirs are castrated. The royal dynasty has been cut short. And worst of all, their temple has been burned to the ground. In exile they sit down by the river and weep, saying, "How can we sing the LORD's song in a foreign land?" (Ps 137:4). It is in this context that the author of Genesis 1 says: *Don't you see? The whole earth is YHWH's temple. And it's all very good!*

The same image runs through the second myth as well. We zoom in on one lush garden in the land of Eden. We don't get much detail about this garden, but, as we've seen, at its center there is a tree of life. This tree is the embodiment of YHWH's life-giving power. In fact, it is so powerful that if someone eats from it, they will "live forever" (Gen 3:22). No one in the story is permitted to eat from this tree, but there are four rivers flowing out of it, spreading the life-giving power of YHWH throughout the world.

The connections don't end there. If Genesis 1 imagines the creatures of the cosmos participating in the divine act of creation, Genesis 2 kicks this image into overdrive. Humanity, in this story, is a gardener. And like all gardeners, these first humans are tasked with "keeping" (*shamar*, Gen 2:15) the land, assisting in the flourishing of creation. But if Genesis 1 is correct, if all creation is a temple, then these gardeners are, at the same time, workers tending the temple of YHWH. They are, in a word, priests—those tasked with "keeping" (*shamar*, Lev 22:9) YHWH's rituals and ordinances.[10] As far as Genesis 1 and 2 are concerned, human beings are created to be gardener-priests, idols and representatives of the divine, tasked with cultivating the flourishing of all creation by extending to it the life-giving

---

10. On the temple imagery in the Eden story, see esp. Wenham, "Sanctuary Symbolism in the Garden of Eden." Wenham points out, among other things, that the two words "tend/work/service" and "guard/protect/keep" only occur together in the Bible when used of priests and of Adam in this story, suggesting that Adam is presented as akin to a priest.

divine energy, around which the whole world "lives and moves and has its being" (Acts 17:28).[11]

A cosmic temple, tended to by gardener-priests—we almost have the whole picture in our minds. But there's one last piece of this puzzle that we need. Or rather, there is one piece of the puzzle that we probably have to swap out. When you read about the garden of Eden, what kind of landscape do you picture? A rough-and-tumble backyard garden? An urban plot? Sweeping fields of agricultural land? When I (Justin) ask my students this question, many of them imagine something like a lush rainforest jungle. But then I ask them to consider a key detail: there are four rivers that each are said to flow out from the center of the garden. How is that possible? How can four rivers flow out of one place? Usually at this point, one visually gifted student will raise her hand and offer a suggestion, "is it . . . a mountain?" That's right! There's only one topography in which four rivers can flow out from a center point—a mountain.

The idea of a mountain-garden isn't as strange as it might seem. Large, tiered gardens—built on a ziggurat to resemble a mountain—were well-known in the ancient Near East. The Assyrian king Sennacherib constructed a vast tiered garden, watered by elaborate aqueducts and shockingly sophisticated engineering mechanisms to pump water to the top. Indeed, this was probably the real-world ancient wonder that would later be misnamed the "Hanging Gardens of Babylon." Genesis 2 draws from this same symbol set.

And so, if the Genesis 1 poem introduced the idea of creation as a temple, now in Genesis 2, we see that it is something even more majestic: *a cosmic temple-mountain.* This isn't just some garden in a long-forgotten land of Eden, this is the Jewish equivalent of the Tibetan Mount Kailash or the Greek Mount Olympus. Eden was a cosmic mountain because the mountaintop is a boundary point, the place where the heavens and the earth collide. Eden is where the domain of YHWH and the domain of humans overlap. In the words of the prophet Ezekiel: "you were in Eden, the garden of God; . . . I placed you on the holy mountain of God" (Ezek 28:13–14).

---

11. To borrow a line from the author of Acts of the Apostles, whose author himself borrowed it from the Cretan poet Epimenides of Knossos.

A TRAGICALLY IRONIC POST-SCRIPT

The tree of life is not alone in the center of this cosmic temple-mountain. There is another tree—the tree of the knowledge of good and evil. This second tree represents the entrance into the full consciousness of a moral universe. Adam is commanded not to eat from this tree: "you may freely eat of every tree of the garden, but of the tree of the knowledge of good and evil you shall not eat, for in the day that you eat of it you shall die" (Gen 2:16–17). But under the influence of a mysterious serpent, the humans ignore this divine injunction and seize the fruit of this forbidden tree. In that moment, they are thrust from the safety of the divine womb and become conscious of a separateness from YHWH, from each other, and from the earth.

In this decisive act, Adam and Eve seek to become "like god" (Gen 3:4). The tragic irony here is that they are grasping for something that they already have. We've heard the words of YHWH on the sixth day: "let us make humans in our image" (Gen 1:26). Adam and Eve attempt to seize divine likeness, misunderstanding the deeper truth: they are *already* "like god." For YHWH, divine likeness isn't something to be jealously guarded, but something to be creatively shared. In the words of an early Christian hymn:

> Though he existed in the form of God,
>   [Christ] did not regard equality with God
>   as something to be grasped,
> but emptied himself,
>   taking the form of a slave,
>   assuming human likeness. (Phil 2:6–7)

The natural reverberation of this tragic misstep is death. The first life lost is an innocent animal whose hide is used to cover their shame (as they discover their nudity). Exiled from the garden, they carry this death with them. It quickly begins to infect the whole world. Adam and Eve are living, breathing idols of YHWH, divine image-bearers, gardener-priests tasked with extending life-giving energy to the whole of creation. But humans so often forget . . .

2

Hermon
The Mountain of Cosmic Revolt

AT THE THREE-WAY BORDER between Syria, Lebanon, and the Israeli-occupied Golan Heights sits Mount Hermon. Today, this mountain range is home to a large nature reserve and ski resort. But this picturesque image of winter recreation is marred by the presence of the highest permanently manned United Nations position in the world. Colloquially known as "Hermon Hotel," this brutally cold position is staffed by Nepalese peacekeeping forces working on behalf of the UN Disengagement Observer Force. The position serves as an early warning system and relies on the height of the peak to spot potential hostilities related to the Israeli occupation of the Golan Heights and the nearby Palestinian West Bank.

This very real human conflict echoes an older tradition of mythical conflict emanating from this same mountain. For, according to *1 Enoch*, it is on the peak of Mount Hermon that a company of rebelling divine beings first forged a plot against YHWH and against humankind.

GENERATION OF WICKEDNESS

Cosmic revolt from above is mirrored by human violence below. This catastrophic chain of events begins precisely where the previous chapter concluded: the death of an animal to cloak humanity's shame. This is only the first innocent blood that is going to be spilled. If Adam and Eve stumbled upon death through a tragic misstep, their first-born, Cain, sought it out intentionally—murdering his brother Abel in cold blood.

Abel, we are told, is "a keeper of sheep," while Cain is "a tiller of the ground" (Gen 4:2). In due time, each brings his respective sacrifice to YHWH. Cain brings the fruit of the soil and Abel the firstlings of his flock. For reasons that are not specified in the text, YHWH rejects Cain's sacrifice in favor of Abel's. Many explanations have been given for this preference: perhaps YHWH prefers a blood sacrifice; perhaps Abel brought the first-born—and therefore most valuable—part of his flock, while Cain did not. It is ultimately unclear. What matters is Cain's response. Faced with rejection and humiliation, Cain invites his brother into a field and beats him to death. Once again innocent blood has been spilled. Abel's blood cries out from the ground for justice. So YHWH curses Cain from the earth and sends him wandering east, further into exile.

In the east, Cain establishes a city and begins to grow his family. Within a few generations, Cain's descendent, a brutal man named Lamech, introduces polygamy into the world and boasts of his excessive violence:

> Adah and Zillah, hear my voice;
> > you wives of Lamech, listen to what I say:
> I have killed a man for wounding me,
> > a young man for striking me.
> If Cain is avenged sevenfold,
> > truly Lamech seventy-sevenfold. (Gen 4:23–24)

Rather than the life-giving waters of the garden, it is violence and terror that now pour out of Eden—consuming and destroying everything in their wake as they sweeps across the world. Creation is coming undone and chaos is bursting forth across the land. Watching this violence increase generation after generation, YHWH mourns that "the wickedness of humans was great in the earth." Indeed, YHWH regrets creating humans and is grieved in Their heart (Gen 6:5–6).

THE SONS OF GOD

The generations of Cain are not the only vantage point from which to view the revolt against YHWH. In the biblical worldview, events that take place here on earth are often understood as reflections of unseen occurrences in the heavenly realms. For example, when the prophet Isaiah says he will make a "taunt against king of Babylon" (Isa 14:4), the taunt he makes is actually about the casting down of some heavenly being called the "Morning Star, son of Dawn," who says to himself "I will ascend to the tops of the clouds; I will make myself like the Most High" (14:12–14). Similarly, the ouster of the king of Tyre mirrors the exile of an angelic being who had been given the task of guarding Eden (Ezek 28). So, if Cain's descendants are in open rebellion against YHWH, we should expect to see some heavenly hijinx as well. The text does not disappoint. For, as human evil spreads across the land, a group of spiritual beings known as the "sons of god" launch a revolt in the heavens (Gen 6:1–2). The human rebellion below mirrors the cosmic rebellion above.

The biblical text shows us only glimpses of the heavenly revolt. In the opening words of the narrative, we are told: "when people began to multiply on the face of the ground, and daughters were born to them, the sons of god saw that they were fair, and they took wives for themselves of all that they chose" (Gen 6:1–2). These sons of god are a mysterious group of spiritual beings who periodically appear in the biblical texts under a variety of names, including: gods, sons of god, the host of heaven, and watchers. In the Semitic idiom of the day, "son of" meant "one of the same type." Sons of god, therefore, simply means gods or deities.

Many people think of the Bible as a monotheistic document in which YHWH is the only divine being. But this simply isn't true. Like every good monarch, YHWH is presented as holding a royal court, in this case consisting of other gods: "God has taken his place in the divine council; in the midst of the gods he holds judgment" (Ps 82:1). YHWH is not the only god in the biblical world, but They are the highest of the gods. And for the Hebrews, They alone are to be worshiped.

> Let the heavens praise your wonders, O LORD,
>   your faithfulness in the assembly of the holy ones.
> For who in the skies can be compared to the LORD?
>   Who among the [sons of god][1] is like the LORD,
> a God feared in the council of the holy ones,
>   great and awesome above all who are around him? (Ps 89:5–7)

The sons of god are in YHWH's employ. Thus, the book of Job begins with an account of the sons of god presenting themselves before YHWH, and

---

1. The NRSVue here renders *bnei Elohim* as "heavenly beings," which is conceptually accurate as the phrase seems primarily to be a signifier of heavenly dwelling. But we have placed in brackets the more literal translation, "sons of god."

of YHWH calling one of them—a god here identified only by his title, "the accuser"—to give an account of his whereabouts.

> One day the [sons of god] came to present themselves before the LORD, and the accuser also came among them. The LORD said to the accuser, "Where have you come from?" The accuser answered the LORD, "From going to and fro on the earth and from walking up and down on it." (Job 1:6–7)

YHWH uses the council to do his bidding throughout the world. For instance, when the wicked Israelite king Ahab and his wife Jezebel fabricate evidence in order to incite a lynch mob against their neighbor, YHWH decides it is time for them to be removed from office (1 Kgs 21:1–16). YHWH thinks that starting a war will be the most efficient way to take care of Ahab, but They need assistance getting Ahab to commit to the conflict. The prophet Micaiah reports this uniquely disturbing scene of the backroom machinations of the divine council:

> I saw the LORD sitting on his throne, with all the host of heaven standing beside him to the right and to the left of him. And the LORD said, "Who will entice Ahab, so that he may go up and fall at Ramoth-gilead?" Then one said one thing, and another said another, until a certain spirit came forward and stood before the LORD, saying, "I will entice him." (1 Kgs 22:19–21)

YHWH wants to know how the spirit plans to carry out the task. "I will go out and be a lying spirit in the mouth of all his prophets," the spirit replies. YHWH confirms, "Go out and do it" (1 Kgs 22:22).

The role of the sons of god in the biblical narrative is not merely advisory. Each is given unique jurisdiction over a certain area of creation. In Deuteronomy 32, YHWH divides the nations among the gods:

> Remember the days of old;
>   consider the generations long past.
> Ask your father and he will tell you,
>   your elders, and they will explain to you.
> When the Most High gave the nations their inheritance,
>   when he divided all mankind,
> he set up boundaries for the peoples
>   according to the number of the [sons of god].[2]

---

[2]. Some translations, including the NRSV, use the alternate reading: "sons of Israel." But apart from "sons of Israel" making little narrative sense, "sons of god" is attested by both the Masoretic text and early fragments such as the Dead Sea Scrolls. On this point, see: Heiser, *Unseen Realm*, 113; Heiser, "Deuteronomy 32:8 and the Sons of God."

> For the LORD's portion is his people,
> Jacob his allotted inheritance. (Deut 32:7-9)

Here, YHWH distributes reign over the various nations of the earth to the sons of god. Each is given authority within their own limited domain. However, Jacob—that is, the Hebrew people or the nation of Israel—is retained by YHWH as Their own portion; a people who will be directly ruled by the creator.

Accordingly, the Hebrews are commanded to remain exclusively loyal to YHWH. They are not to worship these lesser spiritual beings: "when *you* look up to the heavens and see the sun, the moon, and the stars, all the host of heaven, do not be led astray and bow down to them and serve them, things that the LORD your God has allotted to all the peoples everywhere under heaven" (Deut 4:19). The nations might worship these other gods who have been assigned to them, but the Israelites are to worship YHWH alone.

Unfortunately, the sons of god fail to justly govern the lands over which they are given dominion. They seek to hoard power for themselves; they rule without justice; they oppress the weak and the powerless. And so YHWH ultimately condemns them:

> God has taken his place in the divine council; in the midst of the gods he holds judgment: "How long will you judge unjustly and show partiality to the wicked? Give justice to the weak and the orphan; maintain the right of the lowly and the destitute. Rescue the weak and the needy; deliver them from the hand of the wicked." (Ps 82:1-4)

When sons of god rebuff this judgment, YHWH's threat is not subtle: "you are gods, children of the Most High, all of you; nevertheless, you shall die like mortals and fall like any prince" (Ps 82:6-7).

The rebellious councilors of YHWH have abandoned their place and their role in order to seize coercive power by—like the human rebel Lamech—seizing women in an act of sexual violence. Beyond that, the biblical text gives us tantalizingly little detail.

COSMIC CONSPIRACY

While we get only a glimpse of this drama in the Tanakh, ancient Jewish communities were deeply interested in exploring and expanding this strange story. They wanted to understand what the sons of god were up to and how it was linked to human wickedness. In the period following the completion of the Tanakh, Jewish authors began to compose texts that expanded upon this narrative. These texts—including *1 Enoch*, *The Book of Giants*, and *Jubilees*—would become hugely influential on many strains within Second Temple Judaism, including early Christianity. In fact, the New Testament books of 2 Peter and Jude both make direct reference to *1 Enoch*.

All of these expositions on the sons of god are classic apocalypses. But unlike the way that term gets thrown around today, they do not deal with planet-killing asteroids, zombie pandemics, or some other end-of-the-world scenario. Rather, *apocalypse* simply means "to reveal" or "to unveil." In these classic Jewish apocalypses, a figure is granted unique access to divine knowledge. Often it comes to them on a heavenly journey wherein the hidden truth of reality is unveiled before their eyes. In the case of *1 Enoch*, it is the titular Enoch who is given this special knowledge. Enoch is unique in the Bible because he is, together with Elijah, one of only two people to be taken to the heavens without experiencing death: "Enoch walked with God; then he was no more, because God took him" (Gen 5:24). The ancient author(s) of *1 Enoch* latched onto this miraculous assumption and used Enoch's trip into the heavenly realm as a framing device to unpack the mystery of the sons of god.

The core of this angelic revelation is an expansion of the brief Genesis 6 narrative. Borrowing language from the book of Daniel, it refers to the sons of god as "watchers" (see Dan 4). The watchers in this Second Temple literature have a strict military hierarchy. At the helm of the rebellion is Shemihazah, the traitorous leader of the watchers, who would later serve as a model for Christian narratives of Lucifer. Shemihazah has nineteen lieutenants, who together lead a force of 180 watchers. On the peak of Mount Hermon, these rebels make a pact to abandon their place in the heavenly council and descend upon the earth and take human wives. In this way, the sons of god attempt to illegitimately bridge the gap between the heavens and earth *from above*. Like Adam and Eve seizing the fruit in the garden, the sons of god abandon their own domain and descend into the world to seize human women for themselves and on their own terms.

A GIANT PROBLEM

The book of Genesis provides little detail about the rebellion of the sons of god or their sexual exploits. We are told only that "the Nephilim were on the earth in those days—and also afterward—when the sons of god went into the daughters of humans, who bore children to them" (Gen 6:4). The illicit sexual liaison between the sons of god and human women produces a half-human, half-divine race called the Nephilim (also known as Rephaim and Anakim), who will later be described as ferociously aggressive giants (1 En. 7).

This sort of myth strains the credulity of the modern reader. But notice how this narrative intervenes in the religious polemics of its time. Mediterranean and Mesopotamian societies regularly sought to justify their political and social power by retrojecting myths of semi-divine founding figures—Gilgamesh, Hercules, Marduk, etc. These "heroes of old, warriors of renown" (Gen 6:4), are often described not only as courageous and effective warrior-kings but also as physically enormous and powerful beings. The temple Etemenanki at Babylon—the real-life ziggurat that likely inspired the narrative of the Tower of Babel (see below)—housed a massive bed, thirteen-and-a-half feet long, supposedly fit for the giant Marduk.

While other ancient societies told these stories to legitimize their authority, the Hebrew authors turn the narratives on their heads. They don't deny the size and power of their neighbors' primeval kings. Instead, they write the characters into their own narrative—no longer as the possessors of a unique divine favor, but as the product of a divine rebellion and sexual violence. This polemic can often be quite direct. *The Book of Giants*, found in pieces among the Jewish Dead Sea Scrolls, for example, includes both Gilgamesh and Utnapishtim (key characters in the Babylonian *Epic of Gilgamesh*) among the list of Nephilim. In the hands of Jewish authors writing during, or in living memory of, the Babylonian exile, these giant-kings became symbols of chaos and violence, rather than of divine blessing.

Like a corrupted Prometheus the watchers and their offspring grant humans the forbidden knowledge of magic, sorcery, and the skills to craft weapons of war. Power and violence become systematized. The Nephilim are a reification of the consequences of unconstrained power. They spread across the land consuming everything. And when they run out of food, they turn on their human servants and cannibalistically devour them, too. Chaos is spreading through creation, and it is now quite literally consuming itself. The symbolism isn't particularly subtle here: power, violence, and war always cannibalize the very communities they are supposed to protect.

Such evil cannot be permitted to spread unchecked. And so YHWH commissions three archangels—Raphael, Gabriel, and Michael—to put down the watcher rebellion and destroy their monstrous offspring (*1 En.* 10).

In the heavenly realm, the watchers are cast into a cosmic prison, where Enoch is sent to proclaim a message of uncompromising divine judgment against the traitors: "you will have no peace or forgiveness" (*1 En.* 12:4). By the time the New Testament will be written, this story is so well known that 1 Peter can reiterate it, substituting Jesus for the role of Enoch. And so, according to this letter, Jesus spends that first Holy Saturday visiting the watchers in their prison in order to proclaim their judgment: "he went and made a proclamation to the spirits in prison, who in former times did not obey, when God waited patiently in the days of Noah" (1 Pet 3:19–20).

In the earthly realm, the first wave of giants is destroyed by a global flood and later clans are systematically exterminated by the great Hebrew leaders (Gen 14; Num 13; Deut 2–3; Josh 15; 1 Sam 17). But evil is not so easily eradicated. According to the non-canonical Jewish literature, the spirits of these giants were "unclean," because of their mixed divine/human lineage. So, they are not permitted to rest in *sheol*—the Jewish realm of the dead. Instead, the spirits of these dead giants are cursed to wander the earth forever, continuing to inspire evil (*1 En.* 15:7–9). The New Testament knows these spirits by a different name: demons. Within the narrative context of the Bible, Jesus' various exorcisms and conflicts with unclean spirits are a continuation of this cosmic conflict. Jesus culminates the tradition of the Hebrew patriarchs by contending with these monstrous beings.

THE COUNTER-EDEN

The Enochic telling of the sons of god narrative includes one last key detail absent from Genesis: the rebellion is launched from Mount Hermon (*1 En.* 6:5). In biblical history, Moses and the Israelites defeat a king named Og of Bashan, who ruled over Mount Hermon (Num 21:21–35; Deut 3:1–11; Josh 12:4–5). Unsurprisingly, King Og is said to be among the last of the Rephaim—a clan of watcher-descended giants. Undoubtedly, this connection is central to the narrative decision to portray Hermon as the site from which Shemihazah and the watchers launched their rebellion.

But this is not the only reason Mount Hermon is theologically significant. For the indigenous people of the region, the peaks of Hermon carry deep religious significance as the home of Baal, a deity found in various forms among the Canaanites, Phoenicians, and other Levantine peoples. For the Jews, the north (including Bashan and Mount Hermon) became synonymous with foreign deities, idolatry, and religious apostasy.

If Eden is the mountain of divine co-creativity, the place where the heavens and the earth are brought together and where divine and human energies align in service of love and justice—then Hermon is the anti-Eden. It is the symbol of every attempt to seize coercive power. To borrow an image from the psalmist, Hermon can only look with envy at the real mountain of YHWH.

> O mighty mountain, mountain of Bashan;
> O many-peaked mountain, mountain of Bashan!
> Why do you look with envy, O many-peaked mountain,
> at the mount that God desired for his abode,
> where the LORD will reside forever? (Ps 68:15–16)

A GLOBAL CATACLYSM

In the midst of this human and cosmic rebellion, a man named Noah—the great-grandson of Enoch—has a strange encounter. Perhaps it's a dream? Maybe a vision? The text doesn't say. But he is given the most terrifying instructions from YHWH. Noah is to build a boat, an ark vast in scale and meticulously constructed. This ark is to be a life raft. For a flood of unprecedented proportions is coming, a truly global cataclysm. Noah's ark is to protect creation itself, by rescuing the creatures of the sixth day of creation—"cattle and creeping things and wild animals of the earth of every kind" (Gen 1:24). Not all the creatures, of course. Along with Noah and his immediate family, only a single pair of every unclean animal and seven pairs of the clean will be saved—the latter will be required for sacrifices. Everyone else, everything else that dwells on the earth, will face the coming torrent with no ark, no protection. A genocide like nothing before or since is coming, and its instigator appears to be YHWH Themselves.

Why? Why would the "god of the living" (cf. Mark 12:27) cause so much death and destruction? Despite millennia of interpretations and justifications, reams of apologetic texts, and countless children's Bibles depicting a grinning Noah standing side-by-side with giraffes—the sheer horror of this narrative cannot be stifled. How many children drown in this flood? How many dogs and cats sink to the bottom of the sea when their paddling legs finally give up? How can such a story possibly sit in the opening pages of a book purportedly about a just, merciful, and loving creator?

We could take the easy route and hide behind the fact that there is no geological or archeological evidence that such a global flood ever occurred. We could dismiss the narrative as mythic fiction and move on. But this only repositions the problem. Even if we reject the faux-literalism that demands we affirm an actual global flood, we still have to ask: What is this flood doing in this narrative? Why would these ancient authors depict YHWH as a moral monster, particularly in a text that otherwise celebrates divine mercy and justice? This is one question to which a narrative reading of the Bible must respond.

UNCREATION AND RECREATION

The global flood of Genesis 6–7 is the narrative figure of a world come apart. If Eden was a hinge-point—the place where the heavens and the earth came together—the flood is creation come unhinged. The flood isn't punishment; it's consequence. The life-giving link between the heavens and the earth has been severed by human and divine revolt. And so, creation is running backward; the chaotic deep of Genesis 1:2 is bursting forth into the firmament. The flood is the reification of generations of murder, coercion, and sexual violence. The flood is undoing creation; it is Mount Hermon; it is anti-Eden.

But the flood is not the end of the story. In the midst of this cataclysmic storm floats Noah and his ark. This ark will come to rest atop another mountain—not Eden, but not Hermon either.

> God remembered Noah and all the wild animals and all the domestic animals that were with him in the ark. And God made a wind blow over the earth, and the waters subsided; the fountains of the deep and the windows of the heavens were closed, the rain from the heavens was restrained, and the waters gradually receded from the earth. At the end of one hundred fifty days the waters had abated, and in the seventh month, on the seventeenth day of the month, the ark came to rest on the mountains of Ararat. The waters continued to abate until the tenth month; in the tenth month,

on the first day of the month, the tops of the mountains appeared. (Gen 8:1–5)

Below the mountains of Ararat, the flood waters ebb. The boundary between the waters above and the waters below is re-established as dry land reappears.

On the top of this mountain, YHWH establishes a partnership with Noah, his family, and with all creation. YHWH knows that humanity will continue to choose coercive power instead of co-creativity. Evil will return; "for the inclination of the human heart is evil from youth" (Gen 8:21). But YHWH promises: "never again shall all flesh be cut off by the waters of a flood, and never again shall there be a flood to destroy the earth" (Gen 9:11). While "I will never destroy you ... *with a flood*" might seem to offer a rather wide caveat, the narrative and symbolic point is essential. The promise to Noah is not merely that YHWH will never destroy with water, but that YHWH will not allow the earth to return to the chaotic deep. Never again will creation be undone. There will be no more cosmic resets, no more do-overs. YHWH and humanity will have to find a way to make this complicated relationship work.

COUNTERFEIT COSMIC MOUNTAIN

This promise is good news because human violence returns, and it returns fast. Noah builds a garden on Mount Ararat—a new garden on the mountain of re-creation—an Eden 2.0. But he uses the garden to invent alcohol and go on the world's first recorded bender. In his drunken stupor, Noah passes out naked and his son Ham sees "the nakedness of his father" (Gen 9:22). While the meaning of this euphemism is unclear, it almost certainly refers to some sort of sexual violence against Noah or his wife. Echoing Eden, the harmony of Ararat fractures into discord and violence.

Like the violence and power dynamics that infected Eden, those that overtook Ararat spiral out of control. The people move to the east. They invent bricks and begin to build a tower of their own design: "Come, let us build ourselves a city and a tower with its top in the heavens, and let us make a name for ourselves" (Gen 11:4). But this is no skyscraper. We would recognize it as a stepped-pyramid, a ziggurat. It is a temple whose shape is unmistakable: *they are building their own counterfeit cosmic mountain*. In imitation of the watchers at Hermon, humans attempt to bridge the gap between the heavens and the earth, this time *from below*. They have constructed a place where they can seize control of the manifestation of the divine and "make a name" for themselves. They carry the hubris of Lamech and the ambition of the watchers.

Because of the way this passage has been translated into English, the tower is known to history as Babel. But in the Hebrew original it has another name: Babylon. The epitome of human hubris is narrativized as the birth of the very same empire that will one day conquer and destroy the Jewish people and wage war on the mountain-temple of YHWH. At Babel, the destructive spirit of Babylon takes root.

This is how mythology works: something as mundane as building a tower and something as cosmic as angelic-human hybrids are symbols of the same ambition, violence, and war. For the mythicists of Genesis, humans have a choice between two ways of life—one of divine co-creativity and one of seizing coercive power. There are two types of temple-mountains: we can dwell on Eden, the mountain of YHWH's peace, or on Hermon, the mountain of the watchers' violence; on Ararat, the mountain of renewed creation, or on Babel, the mountain of human hubris.

Narratively, YHWH's response to Babel is swift. The tower is destroyed and the people are scattered. But the reality can't be ignored. Within a few short generations, things have already degraded to the same wickedness that preceded the flood. But now YHWH has promised that They will never again allow the chaotic waters to overtake creation. YHWH is committed to finding a way to work with the people They allotted as Their own portion, to bring the creation project back on track. And so YHWH looks to the land of Ur of the Chaldeans, to a man named Abraham and his wife, Sarah.[3]

---

3. At this point in the story, they actually go by their birth names, Abram and Sarai, respectively. Later YHWH will change their names to Abraham and Sarah. But for simplicity, we refer to them as Abraham and Sarah throughout.

3

Moriah
The Mountain of Sacrifice

WHILE THE COSMIC MOUNTAINS of ancient texts generally pointed to real peaks, it is often difficult to discern their present-day location. Mount Moriah presents a paradigmatic case of this difficulty. Both ancient sources and modern scholars have proposed a variety of sites for this famous peak. Muslim theologians have traditionally located this mountain south of ancient Israel, on the Arabian Peninsula, close to Mecca. This southern slide sits well with the Muslim interpretation of the Moriah narrative. In the Quranic telling, it is Ishmael—the first son of Abraham and mythical ancestor of the Arabs—rather than Isaac, the mythical ancestor of the Jews, who takes center stage.

In a similar (though geographically inverse) manner, the Samaritans shifted the narrative north to their homeland, onto Mount Gerizim, in the modern-day Palestinian West Bank. For the Samaritans, Mount Gerizim is the ultimate cosmic mountain, the center of divine presence and power. Today, more than half of the approximately nine hundred remaining Samaritans live in a small village directly adjacent to this mountain.

The most common consensus of Moriah's location is Jerusalem, the site of the temple of Solomon, on the hill known elsewhere as Mount Zion (see chapter 5). This tug of war exemplifies the impact and resonance of the stories of Moriah. Three distinct religious communities seek to locate these events at the symbolic heart of their spiritual and cultural lives.

Not far from Mount Moriah, Abraham wakes up early in the morning to cut firewood and prepare his donkey for travel. He takes his son, Isaac, and two young slaves, and heads off into the wilderness. After a three-day journey, Moriah's peak finally begins to materialize in the distance. Abraham commands the slaves to stay with the donkey and to set up camp. He and Isaac will go to the mountain to worship, he says, and then will return.

When they scale the mountain, Abraham sets to work building an altar out of stone. He arranges wood on the altar for a burnt offering. Once all the preparations have been made, Abraham grabs his son by the arm and begins to bind him. What perhaps at first seems like playful wrestling quickly turns into a horrific nightmare as Abraham binds the boy and presses him onto the altar. Jagged points of firewood cut into his back. Whether Abraham has gagged his son or just endures his screams, the text does not say. Holding his child down with a stiff arm, Abraham—the chosen vessel of YHWH's mercy—draws a dagger from his cloak with his free hand and raises it above his head, ready to plunge it into his son's chest.

SMASHING THE GODS

When YHWH commands Abraham, "Take your son, your only son Isaac . . . and offer him there as a burnt offering" (Gen 22:2), Abraham doesn't ask for further instruction. He knows how to arrange an altar for human sacrifice. Is there a proper incantation to say before burning your child as an offering? Abraham doesn't have to ask. He already knows.

Ancient Judaism didn't appear out of thin air. Like every other religious tradition, it evolved within a specific socio-cultural context—in this case, ancient Canaanite religion. We already saw in the last chapter that even as the Hebrew people committed to worship YHWH alone, they retained echoes of their polytheistic forebears—in the complex figures of the sons of god. We also know that some Canaanites practiced a form of ritualistic child sacrifice. So, it is not surprising that Abraham is acquainted with the practice. But Abraham is beginning to forge his own spiritual path.

When YHWH calls Abraham to "Go from your country and your kindred and your father's house to the land that I will show you" (Gen 12:1), it isn't like a young adult heading off to college or their first career.[1] The challenge is to leave the community, which, in the absence of any centralized governance, provides all basic social welfare and security. It is to quit

---

1. See 23n3 above.

The Cosmic Mountain

the family business, to leave the family land that stood as a sort of ancient pension. Most of all, it is to leave behind the family gods and goddesses, to renounce the ancestral religion, and step into a brand-new way of imagining the world.

According to rabbinic lore, Abraham's father, Terah, was a maker and seller of idols. There's a tale—which appears in both Jewish midrash and the Qur'an—that before he set off for that far country, Abraham went into his father's statuary where the family gods and goddesses were kept and smashed all of the statues to bits with a wooden staff, save for the biggest one. He then slid the wooden staff into the hands of that remaining statue. When Terah returned to discover his inventory destroyed, he asked "What happened here?"

"Isn't it pretty obvious what happened here?" replied Abraham with a wink. "The greatest god has destroyed all the others."

"Are you making fun of me?" Terah demanded, furiously. "These statues aren't alive. They're made of wood, stone, and bronze. I built them myself."

"Do you even hear what you're saying?" Abraham asked in reply. The implication is clear: if you made them with your own hands, then why do you bow to them?[2] Mic drop.

In exchange for the loss of his current family, YHWH promises to make Abraham's new family grow into a great nation: "I will bless you and make your name great, so that you will be a blessing. I will bless those who bless you, and the one who curses you I will curse, and in you all the families of the earth shall be blessed" (Gen 12:2–3). Notice how Abraham is chosen not for his own sake, but for the sake of everyone else. It's as though that life-giving divine energy that flowed out from the center of the garden-temple will now flow from the family that YHWH has promised to Abraham. This is the structure of election in the Bible: some are chosen, not at the expense of others, *but for the sake of others*.[3]

If you're going to become a great nation, you need descendants and you need a land for them to dwell in. But when he gives up everything to set off on this unknown journey, Abraham has neither. He doesn't have so much as a plot to pitch a tent on. And lacking a son, even the tent would be bequeathed to one of his slaves. Year after year there remains no sign

---

2. See Midrash *B'reishit Rabbah* 38.13; Qur'an 21.51–70.

3. The definitive discovery of this structure of the doctrine was made by the twentieth-century theologian, Karl Barth is his *Church Dogmatics* II/2.

that YHWH will keep Their promise. So, when YHWH appears to Abraham again in a vision and says "I am your shield; your reward shall be very great," Abraham has some choice words for Them: "What will you give me, for I continue childless? ... You have given me no offspring, so a slave born in my house is to be my heir" (Gen 15:1–3).

YHWH's response is to lead Abraham outside and instruct him to "look toward heaven and count the stars. ... So shall your descendants be," YHWH promises (Gen 15:5). Oddly, this visionary exchange seems to have taken place just before dusk (see Gen 15:12), which means that YHWH took Abraham outside to count the stars in broad daylight. This subtle detail, dropped by a masterful writer, indicates that Abraham is being asked to believe in promises yet to be fulfilled, to count stars he cannot see.

BRING ME A HEIFER

Abraham asks what anyone in his situation might ask: "How am I to know?" (Gen 15:8). What reason does Abraham have to believe this unfamiliar deity—this god who, up to this point, has done nothing but make empty promises?

YHWH's response to Abraham's query is somewhat less predictable: "Bring me a heifer," They say. Weird response. YHWH wants not only a very specific three-year-old heifer but also "a female goat three years old, a ram three years old, a turtledove, and a young pigeon" (Gen 15:9). Is this menagerie supposed to allay Abraham's misgivings?

To the original ancient Near Eastern audience of this story, this would have seemed like a totally natural response to Abraham's distrust. YHWH is asking Abraham to enter into a *covenant*. In modern English, the word covenant has taken on a specifically religious connotation. Not so in its original context. In Abraham's world, the covenant (*berith*, in Hebrew) was the standard form of a business merger, prenuptial agreement, or political alliance. If you needed to be able to trust someone to hold up their end of a bargain, you'd make a *berith*.

Today, we'd have a contract like that notarized so that there are enforceable legal ramifications for not keeping your word. But in Abraham's day, in the absence of a more formalized legal system, they resorted instead to *ritually significant threats*. Abraham methodically cuts the gathered animals in half, from head to buttocks. The carcasses are then arranged end to end with an aisle down the middle for both parties to walk through, like the world's most horrific red carpet. The idea, very tangibly displayed, is simple: if you don't hold up your end of the bargain then *this will be you!*

Doing it this way is called "cutting a covenant." The notion even finds its way into contemporary English—we talk about "cutting a deal." So Abraham gets the heifer and the female goat, the ram, and a couple of birds. He cuts the mammals in half and arranges them just so. It's a lot of work. And it's a big, bloody mess. He has to stop several times to drive the buzzards away. So when it's all done, the exhausted Abraham falls asleep. As Abraham sleeps, a smoking fire pot appears to him in a dream. This is what theologians call a "theophany"—a manifestation of YHWH's glory.

The word "glory"—in Hebrew, *kabod*—is related to the root *kbd*, which means heavy or weighty. First Samuel tells the story of a priest, Eli, who died from the fall when the chair on which he was sitting broke underneath him, "because he was *a kabad* man"—a heavy man, a weighty man. So when the ancient Hebrews talk about the glory—the *kabod* of YHWH—they're referring to the weightiness of the divine presence, even though there's no-*body*, no-*thing* that can be pointed to or held on to.

I (Joe) remember sleeping at my grandmother's house the night after her funeral. Granny was a serious scrabble player. Her scrabble board was still sitting out on the kitchen table, and the massive Unabridged Webster's Dictionary—"the Scrabble Bible," she called it—which she used to arbitrate challenged words sat on a hutch beside the table, alongside a cookie jar filled with fun-sized Fifth Avenue candy bars. Granny was a voracious reader and read more broadly and eclectically than anyone I have known since. She loved to watch the squirrels and had a collection of porcelain squirrel figurines that friends and family had gifted her over the years. Two of them adorned the bedside table in the room where I slept. There, amid Granny's books and games, licking the chocolate from one of her Fifth Avenue bars off the tips of my fingers, her squirrels staring me in the face, her presence weighed heavy in that place, even though there was no one there, no place you could point to and say, "she's right there." That's glory.

The glory of YHWH is symbolized in the Bible as fire, cloud, smoke, and light. You can sense the writers grasping for images of things that definitively make their presence known and yet cannot be pinned down or held onto. So, YHWH's glory appears in the form of a smoking fire pot and passes between the animals. This is significant. In a traditional *berith*, the weaker party—called the "vassal"—would walk between the split animals. This signified that, if the covenant was broken, they'd be the one facing the sharp edge of the sword. But that's not what happens here. While Abraham sleeps under a tree, YHWH, the creator of the universe, takes the role of the weaker party in the covenant. It's as if to say it doesn't matter whether Abraham keeps the covenant or not. Indeed, Abraham's failure is all but inevitable. But through it all, YHWH will remain faithful to Their covenant promises. They will dispense Their blessing and life-giving energy to the world through the family of Sarah and Abraham.

TAKING AND GIVING

It's a good thing that YHWH has committed to remaining in the relationship even if Sarah and Abraham don't uphold their end of the covenant. Because you barely have to turn the page before they choose the way of coercive power. More than a decade after YHWH's promise, Sarah and Abraham are still childless, so they decide to seize control of the situation for themselves. They concoct a scheme in which Abraham will sleep with one of Sarah's slaves, Hagar, in order to ensure descendants. Just as Eve stood before the tree of the knowledge of good and evil, "*took* of its fruit and ... *gave* some to her husband" (Gen 3:6); so now Sarah "*took* Hagar ... her slave, and *gave* her to her husband" (Gen 16:3).

This pattern will be repeated when Rachel—the wife of Abraham's grandson, Jacob—similarly *takes* her slave and *gives* her to Jacob as a surrogate, and when YHWH's people get impatient waiting in the wilderness for a place to worship, so they *take* their gold jewelry and *give* it to Aaron to be melted down and turned into an idol, seizing control of the plan for worship. This verbal construction—"take and give"—is used time and again by the very subtle writers and editors of the Bible to represent the choice of coercive power over co-creativity. That is, until the Gospel writers invert this language: Jesus *takes* bread and *gives* it to his disciples in an act of generosity. But we are getting ahead of ourselves.

By exploiting their slave, Abraham and Sarah go the way of the sons of god who sexually exploited human women and of the people at Babel who tried to control the reunion of heaven and earth by building a counterfeit cosmic mountain. Abraham and Sarah tried to seize control of YHWH's plan to make Their life-giving energy available to the whole world. And as in every case of taking coercive power, the result is the suffering of the innocent. Abraham and Sarah rape Hagar; they use her body as their baby-making machine.

It is worth pausing here to notice that the text itself doesn't unequivocally condemn Abraham and Sarah's owning a slave. That Hagar's body, sexuality, and reproductive capacities are the property of her masters is simply taken for granted. Slaves fare no better in New Testament epistles, where they are instructed to "be submissive to their masters" (Titus 2:9), regarding them as "worthy of all honor" (1 Tim 6:1). Indeed, they are to do so "with enthusiasm" (Eph 6:7). When we condemn slavery today, we do so in opposition to a straightforward reading of the Bible. But we understand that the human authors of the Bible—bound as they were in a specific cultural and historical context—sometimes got things wrong. A narrative reading allows us to recognize these parts of the Bible for what they are, even as we look for the liberatory thread that runs through the larger story.

When YHWH's promise finally comes to fruition, Sarah conceives a child of her own. Abraham and Sarah name the baby Isaac. Then, no longer finding her useful, they callously cast Hagar and her son Ishmael out into the wilderness to die. But YHWH does not abandon Hagar and Ishmael, like Abraham and Sarah, but saves their lives and establishes a unique covenant with them as well. (Gen. 17:18-21) Indeed, in Islam, it is Ishmael who is the child of promise (Quran 19.54; cf. Hadith 4.583). Hagar's life is a beautiful if heart-wrenching story of YHWH co-conspiring with this oppressed slave girl to make a way out of no way for her survival and flourishing.[4]

RAISED FROM THE DEAD

Sarah and Abraham finally have a child of their own. They've staked their whole lives on this promise. They left home and family for it. They raped and banished for it. They've believed it to the bitter end. And now, when they are laughably old, they finally can see a glimpse of a path forward. They finally have their promised child.

Then YHWH commands Abraham to kill him.

As Abraham stands there on Mount Moriah, dagger raised, poised to take the life of his own son, we are left to contemplate his psychology. How

---

[4]. If you want to dive into Hagar's story and its theological implications, we cannot recommend highly enough Delores Williams, *Sisters in the Wilderness*. It's an extended meditation on Hagar's story through the lens of the continued oppression, suffering, tenacity, and resourcefulness of Black women today. It's also one of the founding documents of womanist theology. It changed the way we read the Bible.

could he obey YHWH's heinous command to kill his own child? Why not say to YHWH: "If you're the child-sacrifice-demanding type, just like the gods and goddesses that I smashed in my father's house, then you're not who I thought you were. I am not interested in your covenant."

What if Abraham had done just that? Maybe Abraham actually failed this test. Perhaps he was supposed to argue with YHWH the way he did just a few chapters earlier when YHWH threatened to destroy the cities of Sodom and Gomorrah, and Abraham pleaded a daring case for them to be spared (see Gen 18:16–33). What happened to *that Abraham?* He'll fight for people he's never met, but when it comes to his own son suddenly he's lost all his pluck?

In his book *Fear and Trembling*, the eighteenth-century Danish philosopher Søren Kierkegaard eulogizes Abraham. Kierkegaard is particularly struck by Abraham's silence throughout this story. Abraham has nothing to say. He can't defend himself, because there is no defense for his action, no explanation to make. By any moral metric, Abraham is a murderer. It must be the case, Kierkegaard concludes, that relation to the divine or "the Absolute," stands somehow outside of and beyond the matrices of moral reasoning—what Kierkegaard called "the teleological suspension of the ethical."[5]

And so, Abraham plunges the dagger toward Isaac's chest. He is prepared to slaughter the child in whom all of his and Sarah's hopes are bound. But like a flash of lighting, the angel of YHWH erupts onto the scene, staying Abraham's hand. Isaac will live. Obeying this horrific command, Abraham has proven his loyalty to YHWH's covenant—but at what cost?

The writer of the New Testament book of Hebrews anachronistically suggests that Abraham knew, in a sense, how the story would end. At least "he considered the fact that God is able even to raise someone from the dead" (Heb 11:19). If Abraham did consider resurrection as an option, he would have been the first Hebrew thinker to have done so by several hundred years. Either way, the story itself gives no indication.

But one thing is certain: In the face of this deadly trial, Abraham discovers the source of life. For as the angel stays his hand, Abraham spots a ram "caught in a thicket by its horns" and offers it as a burnt offering instead of his son (Gen 22:13). Just as in Eden, a tree at the center of a mountain becomes the source of life for Isaac, Sarah, and Abraham. If you're already thinking ahead to the New Testament, when another tree on top of another

---

5. Kierkegaard, *Fear and Trembling/Repetition*.

mountain becomes a source of life for the world, then you're starting to get a handle on how a narrative reading of the Bible works.

This is what it means to be a covenant partner with YHWH: to make the impossible ascent up the mountain of sacrifice and there to discover YHWH's life-giving energy, which brings blessing to the whole world. But things are about to go very wrong for the descendants of Abraham. The promise is going to be put to the test, as the covenant people are enslaved in a foreign land.

4

Sinai

The Mountain of Covenant

LIKE MOUNT MORIAH, THE precise location of the ancient peak known in the biblical text as Mount Sinai has eluded all who hunt for it. Narratively, it should be located on or near the Sinai Peninsula (which itself gets its name from the eponymous mountain). Scholars have scoured the biblical texts to narrow down the location—mapping out references to distances and the lengths of journeys with rulers and compasses, in a desperate search for the sacred locus. All to little avail. The result is that more than a dozen mountains have been candidates for the location, with prominent contenders including Mount Serbal, Mount Catherine, and Jabal Musa (itself commonly called Mount Sinai today).

At the base of this mountain, wherever it might be, two priests of YHWH named Nadab and Abihu—both sons of Aaron, the first high priest—prepare to enter the tabernacle, a sort of mobile temple where YHWH's glory dwells. They are, we will later learn, a bit drunk. Before they enter the tent, they add the necessary incense to their censors and light them. But as they cross into the tent, their fire is deemed "unholy" (Lev 10:1). It is, as the King James Version famously rendered it, a "strange fire." We are never told exactly why the drunk priests' fire is unauthorized. But in response to this fateful misstep, a divine conflagration erupts from the heart of the tabernacle and incinerates them both on the spot.

Moses—their uncle and the leader of the Hebrew community—declares, "This is what the LORD meant when he said, 'Through those who are near me I will show myself holy, and before all the people I will be glorified'" (Lev 10:3). Aaron, their father, remains heartbreakingly silent.

Whatever YHWH is, YHWH is not safe. Their glory manifests as a power that, if approached carelessly, is truly devastating.

A BROTHERS' QUARREL

To make sense of this short narrative, we need to rewind to the closing chapters of Genesis. There we meet a boy named Joseph, the great-grandson of Sarah and Abraham. Joseph is the first of many biblical figures to possess the divine power of dream interpretation. But if he is gifted, Joseph is not particularly street-smart. He constantly inflames his brothers' antagonism by recounting dreams in which they all bow down before him. Eventually, they have enough. Briefly contemplating murder, they settle on beating their brother to a pulp and selling him off to foreign slave traders.

Joseph is now famous for his "amazing technicolor dreamcoat." That image may, in fact, be the result of a mistranslation. The words used to describe Joseph's coat, *ketonet passim*, may just indicate that it had "long sleeves," biblical scholars are not sure. The only other time that particular combination of words is used in the Hebrew Bible is in a harrowing story in which Amnon, the eldest son of King David, rapes his half-sister Tamar, who is said to be wearing a *ketonet passim*, "for this is how the virgin daughters of the king were clothed in earlier times" (2 Sam 13:18). Transgender Bible scholar and theologian Austin Hartke can't help but wonder whether the violence Joseph's brothers will inflict upon him is not a reaction to his gender-bendy affinity for wearing a princess dress and to their father's apparent approval of this practice.[1] It would certainly cohere with the experience of many transgender folks today, who far too often are still victims of hatred and violence. Whatever the reason, it is clear that Joseph is his father's favorite and this contributes to his brothers' antagonism.

Sold to a wealthy family in Egypt, Joseph faces increasing difficulty as he is falsely accused of sexual assault and thrown into prison. In the centuries since, this narrative of unjust accusation has unfortunately been used to silence very real allegations of sexual violence. But this is a complete inversion of the narrative's actual focus. This is a story about how the rich and the powerful abuse the justice system in their own favor. The enslaved Joseph, like many women who report sexual abuse today, can expect little

1. Hartke, *Transforming*, 68–69.

justice from the courts of law, which so often "write oppressive statutes, to turn aside the needy from justice and to rob the poor" (Isa 10:2).

Despite these setbacks, Joseph uses his divine gift of dream interpretation to work his way out of prison and into the good graces of the Egyptian pharaoh. Able to predict a coming famine, Joseph is tasked with coordinating a project to stockpile food in anticipation of the ensuing catastrophe. When the famine arrives, Joseph's family decide to travel to the well-stocked Egypt in search of provisions. There, in the culmination of his dreams so many decades earlier, they bow before their brother, who is now second-in-command of an entire nation. Joseph seeks no retribution against his brothers. Standing in a position of almost supreme authority, he refuses to wield power like a cudgel. Rather, he asks: "Am I in the place of God?" (Gen 50:19) before embracing his brothers in love and offering them forgiveness.

A NEW BABYLON

Joseph's family ends up putting down roots in Egypt, where he had made a comfortable life for them. But as we turn the page to the book of Exodus, four centuries have passed and a new pharaoh has arisen over Egypt. Memory has faded of the strange, dream-interpreting Hebrew, who saved the whole land. Like so many immigrant communities since, Joseph's descendants are now seen as a threat. "Look, the Israelite people are more numerous and more powerful than we," the new pharaoh exclaims, stoking fears of the other. "Let us deal shrewdly with them, or they will increase and, in the event of war, join our enemies and fight against us and escape from the land" (Exod 1:9–10). The pharaoh decides to solve the problem of this growing immigrant community the only way he knows how—with violence.

His first idea is to break the spirit of the Hebrews by enslaving them. The Hebrews are stripped of their freedom and set to the task of building monuments to the glory of the pharaoh, their oppressor.

Biblical literature—and any text that has been passed down orally, for that matter—tends to be largely devoid of particulars. So when seemingly extraneous details do appear, particularly when they appear more than once, readers should take note. The narrative at this point has one such detail. Multiple times we are told that the slaves are to make and bake bricks for these building projects:

> The Egyptians subjected the Israelites to hard servitude and made their lives bitter with hard servitude in mortar and bricks. (Exod 1:13–14)

> You shall no longer give the people straw to make bricks, as before; let them go and gather straw for themselves. But you shall require of them the same quantity of bricks as they have made previously; do not diminish it, for they are lazy. (Exod 5:7–8)

Why do bricks keep recurring in the narrative? It is an oddly specific detail. It indicates that something is happening below the surface.

The astute reader might remember that we have encountered bricks before—in the opening moments of the Babel narrative. There we are told that, in their quest for power, the people said to one another, "'Come, let us make bricks and fire them thoroughly.' And they had brick for stone and bitumen for mortar" (Gen 11:3). Narratively and symbolically, then, bricks link Egypt to Babel. They have become a symbol of human greed and corruption. Egypt, we are alerted by this tiny recurring detail, *manifests the destructive spirit of Babylon*—another example of the violence and terror of coercive power.

Slavery and forced labor are only stopgap measures in the pharaoh's ultimate plan. He intends to destroy the Hebrews entirely. He instructs the Hebrew midwives to kill any male child upon birth. This eliminates the possibility of the Hebrews raising up an army. If there are no men, then—in this patriarchal society—there will be no soldiers. But it does something else, at once more subtle and more insidious. The Hebrews will now have only girl children, who, if they want to get married, will be forced to marry Egyptian men. In ancient Egyptian society, a child is identified by the ethnicity of their father. The children of Hebrew women and Egyptian men will be Egyptians. By killing off the boys, the pharaoh can eliminate the entire Hebrew people within a generation. It is, to use a modern phrase, ethnic cleansing.

But the pharaoh's plan fails. The Hebrew midwives resist his plot, secretly delivering the Hebrew boys and insisting to their superiors that "the Hebrew women are not like the Egyptian women, for they are vigorous and give birth before the midwife comes to them" (Exod 1:19). Furious, the pharaoh decides to take matters into his own hands. He deputizes the Egyptian people with a simple command: throw the Hebrew infant boys into the Nile River to drown.

A HEBREW LIBERATOR

In the heavens, YHWH hears the voices of Their people crying out for justice. YHWH is not a god who sits on the sidelines when one group holds power over another, when they abuse and kill mercilessly. YHWH takes sides. They raise up a liberator to rescue the covenant people, a man by the name of Moses.

Moses is born in the midst of the pharaoh's genocide. His mother and sister cunningly save him by building a small raft (his own tiny ark [*tebat*]!) and floating him down the Nile. Ironically, they are technically obeying the pharaoh's command to throw the infant boys into the river. In a strange twist, Moses ends up being adopted into the pharaoh's household.

We are not given much insight into Moses' royal upbringing. But we are told that as an adult he witnesses an Egyptian slave master beating a Hebrew slave. And so, in a fit of just rage over the plight of his people—a plight that Moses himself was spared only by the cunning audacity of his mother and a bit of good luck—he attacks and kills the slaver. In this moment, Moses can be seen as something of an analog to YHWH Themselves. YHWH is a god devoted to justice and liberation. Despite being regularly praised as "slow to anger" (e.g., Exod 34:6), the narratives sometimes present Them as remarkably short tempered. Indeed, Moses—like Abraham before him—will later have to talk YHWH out of executing the whole Hebrew people (Exod 32:9–14). But we're getting ahead of ourselves.

Now wanted for the murder of an officer, Moses has to flee for his life. He settles into the wilderness of the Midianites, where he becomes a sheep herder. Many years pass. Moses marries and starts a family. One day, while ascending with his sheep into a mountainous region of the wilderness in search of green pastures and freshwater, Moses stumbles upon something strange. First, he sees a bush that is on fire. That alone is not so uncommon in the hot Arabian desert. But with a closer look, Moses notices that the bush refuses to be consumed by the fire. As he observes this strange phenomenon, a voice erupts from this mysterious burning tree, saying, "the place on which you are standing is holy ground" (Exod 3:5). Moses pulls the sandals off his feet. If this is holy ground, he wants to feel it between his toes.

Now, to be on holy ground is to be in the place where the heavens and the earth unite. So, in the wilderness of the Midianites—out, you might say, in the middle of nowhere—Moses encounters a tree . . . on a mountain . . . in the place where heaven and earth unite. *Moses has stumbled into Eden.*

To be clear, the text doesn't say and we aren't suggesting that Moses discovered the site of the ancient garden. Eden isn't a place on a map. Myths operate with a different kind of geography. Eden is anywhere the heavens and the earth intermingle. Moses is in Eden because he is standing face-to-face with the divine. He has encountered a god. And not just any god, but the god of Abraham, Isaac, and Jacob. Having been raised as an Egyptian, Moses finally encounters his family's god, the god of the covenant. Indeed, it is here that Moses demands to learn the name of this god. To this, YHWH responds, "I will be who I will be" (traditionally rendered "I AM WHO I AM") before unveiling that name that we, the readers, already know—YHWH.

Moses leaves this sacred encounter with a job to do. YHWH has heard the cries of the oppressed in Egypt (Exod 3:7) and has selected Moses to spearhead the rescue operation. Like most of us when faced with such an impossibly difficult task, Moses is hesitant to step into the role. He's not a skilled public speaker, he protests. And so YHWH permits Moses' brother, Aaron, to join the team. The task of being YHWH's representative will be split into two roles: ruler and priest. Moses' failure to take up the unified mantle will haunt the biblical text as ruler and priest remain forever a thorn in one another's side. And the Hebrews will never stop envisioning a future when these roles might be reunited.

As Moses returns to Egypt, this time as a liberator of his people, a series of cosmic battles ensue between the god of the Hebrews and the powers of Egypt, both spiritual and physical. These battles take the form of a series of increasingly intense plagues, which reveal the liberative power of YHWH as They seek to redeem the covenant people. One by one, the gods of the Egyptian pantheon are targeted. The Egyptians venerate Hapi, the god of the Nile. The Nile is turned to blood. They worship Ra, the god of the sun. The sun is turned to darkness. They trust in Ma'at, the god of balance. Fire rains from the heavens.

If these plagues represent YHWH's overcoming of the Egyptian pantheon, they also bring profound human casualties. As above, so below. Worse still, they often bring death to the innocent. Water and crops grow scarce and disease spreads. These plagues culminate with a final ruthless attack on the firstborn Egyptian males. The violence of the Egyptians' attempted genocide of Hebrew children has ricocheted back upon them.

But YHWH provides a means of escape for the covenant people. They are to eat a ritual meal, which includes the sacrifice of a lamb. If they mark the doorposts of their houses with the blood of this lamb, then the Destroyer—a mysterious and deadly spiritual being, who enacts YHWH's harsh justice—will pass by the house and the firstborn will be spared. This is *Pesach* (Passover).

It's easy to be repelled by the cruelty of this divine judgment. If YHWH is good, how can They employ the death of children in Their plan for liberation? But it's important to keep the redemptive context in mind, this is a response to slavery and genocide. Closer to our contemporary situation, we might look at the similar violence of abolition. Was the horrific violence of Nat Turner's slave revolt justified? Was John Brown's armed defense of liberty in Kansas moral? Was the civil war by which Haitian slaves freed themselves legitimate? In each instance, innocent blood was spilt. Liberation is never tidy or uncomplicated. And so, while it is difficult—perhaps impossible—to square YHWH's actions with our contemporary moral intuitions, we must not forget that we are witnessing divine justice against slavers. For the ancient authors of this narrative, the evil of the corrupt and violent Egyptian empire justly rebounded to horrific effect. Nevertheless, to this day Jews still spill a bit of wine as they recount the story of the plagues during the Seder meal. Because violence breeds violence and death begets death. Even when enacted against a true enemy, they drain our joy.

Seeing the devastating loss of life throughout his territory, the pharaoh finally relents and tells Moses he will permit the Hebrews to return to their homeland. But the pharaoh is a weak and fickle man. He soon changes his mind and pursues the fleeing slaves with the full force of the Egyptian army, closing in on them at the shore of the Reed Sea.

Empowered by YHWH, Moses lifts up his staff and strikes the sea. In an echo of the creation poem, the seas separate to expose dry land (cf. Gen 1:9), allowing the Hebrews to cross to safety. The army of the pharaoh follows in hot pursuit. Exiting to refuge on the far shore, Moses strikes the sea again and it collapses in on the pursuing Egyptian army, drowning them all. Committed to being a force of chaos and destruction, the army of the pharaoh is consumed by the destructive power of the chaotic waters.

AWE AND TERROR

With the drowning of the pharaoh's army, the people of YHWH are free. But what have they been freed *for*? They have been freed to be the covenant people, the ones through whom YHWH's promise to Sarah and Abraham will be fulfilled: "In you all the families of the earth shall be blessed" (Gen 12:3). So now they must flourish. They must become as numerous as the stars. They must dwell in the promised land. But first, and most importantly, they must go and worship YHWH.

After a three-month trek through the wilderness, where the covenant people consistently reveal the weakness of their trust in YHWH, they finally arrive at Mount Sinai, the mysterious peak where Moses first met YHWH in the burning bush.

In preparation for the arrival of YHWH to the mountain, the Hebrews are to set up a series of limits around it. No one is to step foot on the mountain during the time of preparation. Anyone who crosses the boundary before the appointed time must be put to death. The community ritually wash themselves and abstain from sexual intercourse, which was understood to leave one ritually (not morally) impure. In this way, they consecrate themselves at the same time that they consecrate the mountain. They are preparing for a covenant ceremony.

Upon completion of the consecrating tasks, YHWH's glory descends upon Mount Sinai in all its awful terror. The earth quakes and the mountain is battered by wind and rain as fire and lightning erupt from its belly, like a live volcano engulfed by a thunderstorm. Black smoke billows from the top of the mountain until it is consumed by a dark cloud.

This is not the first time we have encountered YHWH's fiery glory. When Abraham first made a covenant with YHWH, They appeared as a smoking fire pot. At Moses' inaugural encounter, he witnesses a burning bush. The glory of YHWH is magnificent and dangerous. Like a burning sun, it radiates life into the world. But if you stare directly into it without proper protection, it will burn out your eyes. The glory of YHWH is equal parts life-giving and dangerous.

Once the people and the mountain have been properly consecrated and the preparations completed, Moses and Aaron are permitted to ascend the mountain. The ceremony begins with YHWH reciting a series of covenantal regulations that will eventually total 613 commandments. Here we have a covenant that is both new and old. It is a new covenant in which the Hebrew people will be established as a nation, the nation of Israel, but it is also a recommitment of the covenant first given to Abraham so many generations earlier.

A PRIESTLY KINGDOM AND A HOLY NATION

Soon the circle of trust is expanded. Moses and Aaron, along with Nadab and Abihu—whose untimely deaths we recounted at the opening of this chapter—and seventy elders of the community are invited to ascend the mountain. Moses alone may enter the dark cloud; the rest must "worship at a distance" (Exod 24:1). From there they can see that under YHWH's feet is "something like a pavement of sapphire stone, like the very heaven for clearness" (Exod 24:10). Here we are to imagine that they have been—whether literally or symbolically (a distinction that means little to the Scriptures)—transported into the very throne room of YHWH. From his seat atop the mountain, the deity's face and body are hidden in the dark cloud. The only thing visible from the lower position at which the Aaron, Nadab, Abihu, and the elders stand, is YHWH's ottoman.

In the mountain throne room, they eat a feast. It is a ritual meal to commemorate the renewal of the Abrahamic covenant. It's only because this carefully titrated ritual is rightly performed that they may stand so close to the divine presence and live to tell about it. Remember that the rest of the congregation of the Hebrews are standing back from the foot of the mountain, unable even to approach it.

We already know the aim of the Abrahamic covenant: in the covenant people, "all the nations of the earth gain blessing" (Gen 22:18). But it is only here, in this covenant renewal ceremony, that we begin to get a sense of precisely how that will happen. The Hebrews are told that they will be "a priestly kingdom and a holy nation" (Exod 19:6). That is their mission and agenda. That is how they will be a blessing to the nations.

"Holy" means to be set apart for a special task. To make something holy to YHWH is to take something that is mundane and to consecrate it or declare it as unique, to ordain it for a particular role for YHWH. We do this all the time in daily life. You might have fancy china that you use only on special occasions. Or you might have a nice suit reserved for weddings and funerals. If a priest concluded mass, walked out into the hallway, and poured a diet coke into the communion chalice, you'd probably instinctively wince. These objects are "holy"—they've been set apart for certain unique tasks. And so "holy" doesn't necessarily mean magical or supernatural, but it does mean *distinct and significant.*

Therefore, if Israel is to be a holy nation, it too must be set apart for a special purpose. This idea helps to clarify much of the covenant code. Why is YHWH so worried about how people will dress or what they will eat? Is it morally wrong to eat a shrimp cocktail (Lev 11:10)? To wear a polyester-cotton blend (Deut 22:11)? Of course not. But that's not the point. These aren't moral commands. They are ritual regulations aimed at separating the nation of Israel, of visibly distinguishing it from its neighbors, of making it holy—that is, set apart.

The special task for which the Hebrews are set apart is to be a priestly kingdom. A priest is a mediator, standing between a community and its god. A priest functions like a two-way valve: turned one direction, the priest declares the words of their god to the people—whether in the form of commandments, instructions, or prophecies. Turned the other, they represent the worship, hopes, and desires of the people back to their god—through prayers, songs, and liturgies.

To describe Israel as a priestly nation is not to say that every person in the community will be a literal priest—that they will all serve in the temple, preparing ritual sacrifices and offering prayers. They still need farmers and merchants, tax collectors and soldiers. Rather, it means that, collectively, the nation of Israel is going to play this mediating role between YHWH and the other nations. What Aaron is for Israel, Israel will be for the nations. As we saw in chapter 2, when YHWH divided up the nations among the sons of god, They kept Israel as Their own special portion. Now we know why. Israel is set apart to be a mediator.

But something is missing. If Israel is a priestly nation, they are going to need a temple. Where else does a priest attend to a god but in a temple?

THE TABERNACLE: A MOBILE COSMIC TEMPLE-MOUNTAIN

So Moses advances higher up the mountain and deeper into the presence of his god. He enters a place where the glory of YHWH dwells. He enters into the heart of Sinai, the cosmic temple-mountain, to the tree of life. But is there a tree here? The text doesn't actually say there is. But we're on Mount Sinai. This is precisely where Moses first encountered YHWH in the desert, where he encountered the fiery presence of YHWH's glory in the form of a burning bush—a tree. And so as Moses ascends into the heart of YHWH's glory, he thereby ascends at the same time into the heart of Eden.

In this deepest place, he is given building instructions and a pattern for a tabernacle, a tent-like temple directly modeled on YHWH's dwelling place. For YHWH is ready to come down off of the mountain and dwell *with* the people.

It's hard to miss the Edenic imagery of the design. The tabernacle is covered with images of almonds, pomegranates, and other fruit trees. Inside is a menorah, an eight-limbed candelabra made to look like the tree of life, and whose burning oil represents the flaming power of the bush atop Sinai. This tabernacle will be a mobile micro-Eden. It will be the place, like Eden, from whence YHWH's life-giving energy will once again flow out to the whole world.

The construction of the tabernacle is notably different from what we saw at Babel. There, humans build a temple in order to storm the gates of the heavens and seize control of divine power. Here, YHWH has given Moses and the people the pattern of the tabernacle, precisely in order to share co-creative power.

Once the construction of the tabernacle is complete, the dark cloud of YHWH's glory descends the mountain and pours into it. So thick is the cloud that Moses isn't even able to enter the tent. The book of Exodus ends in confusion and aporia. Will the Hebrew people ever be able to safely dwell with YHWH? Will they be able to fulfill their role as a priestly kingdom, mediating YHWH's life-giving energy to the nations?

DWELLING WITH A DANGEROUS GOD

The answer comes in the next book of the Torah, Leviticus—a text too often casually dismissed as nothing more than an outdated list of pointless rules. Leviticus opens with a series of narratives concerned with the process of consecration. YHWH is not content to sit outside of creation, to dwell at a distance. And yet, YHWH's dwelling is not safe for the people. Their world is one of violence and greed, oppression and death. These things cannot stand in the presence of the god of justice and life. And so, if the people of Israel are going to live together with YHWH, they must first undertake a process of purification and preparation.

YHWH's presence is dangerous, but it is also life-giving. It is like a nuclear reactor that provides power for a city. Hospitals, grocery stores, schools, and parks can all get their power from the reaction churning at the heart of this core. It enlivens the community. But if you casually walk into that core, unprepared, it will tear you apart at a molecular level. To enter the presence of this radioactive power, you need to wear the proper clothing and follow the proper safety procedures. Does this mean that the reactor is evil? No. But it is dangerous.

This is precisely why Leviticus is so concerned with ritual operations, priestly vestments, and proper sacrificial procedures. These are not means of appeasing a cruel and arbitrary god. To the contrary, in the ancient mindset in which these texts were written, these are the precautions that permit you to dwell side-by-side with the very author of life—with a good god committed to living together with Their people.

But when these precautions are not observed, when they are casually ignored—just like ignoring the safety precautions in a nuclear reactor—the consequences can be deadly. When the priests Nadab and Abihu drunkenly disregard the proper ritual procedure, they walk straight into an uncontainable power with no protection; and it incinerates them. This is the warning of Leviticus.

Now, having been liberated from slavery and set apart as a priestly nation, Israel must undertake the impossibly difficult task of living out her covenant obligation to bring a blessing to the nations. This, as we will see, is easier said than done.

5

Zion
The Mountain of Divine Dwelling

MOUNT ZION WAS SO central to the life of ancient Israel that, in the Bible, the word "Zion" often refers, not only to the small peak, but to the whole city of Jerusalem or even the entire nation of Israel. Today, Mount Zion refers to Jerusalem's western hill, just outside the walls of the Old City. It is the home of an ancient tomb, which, since the Middle Ages, has been associated with the burial of King David. But, in King David's own time, Mount Zion was the name of Jerusalem's eastern hill, known today as the Temple Mount. This hill was the site of both the First Temple and, after its destruction by the Babylonians, the Second Temple that survived into the first century CE. Six hundred years later, two Muslim holy sites—the Dome of the Rock and the Al-Aqsa Mosque—were constructed on the ruins of these temples. These two mosques remain there today. Because of this complex history, legitimate control of the Temple Mount remains hotly contested, often escalating into open conflict. In September 2000, the Israeli politician Ariel Sharon took a provocative photo-op on the Temple Mount, leading to a series of protests and riots that erupted into the Second Intifada—a five-year period of Palestinian resistance to Israeli occupation.

A few thousand years earlier, King David gazes at Mount Zion from his palace throne in Jerusalem, the recently established center of Israelite religious and political life. The prophet Nathan stands at attention in the throne room as the king unveils his newest plan: "See now, I am living in a house of cedar, but the ark of God stays in a tent" (2 Sam 7:3). On Mount

Zion, David continues, I will build YHWH a palace as grand as my own. That evening, Nathan retreats to prayer and receives a cutting reply from YHWH:

> Are you the one to build me a house to live in? I have not lived in a house since the day I brought up the people of Israel from Egypt to this day, but I have been moving about in a tent and a tabernacle. Wherever I have moved about among all the people of Israel, did I ever speak a word with any of the tribal leaders of Israel, ... saying, "Why have you not built me a house of cedar?" (2 Sam 7:5–7)

David's monarchical ambitions have collided with YHWH's nomadic intimacy. The status of YHWH's dwelling hangs in the balance.

MILK AND HONEY

Tension between YHWH's plan and the covenant people's desire is nothing new, emerging already in the desert of Sinai. As the migrating community draws near the land that was promised to their forefather Abraham, Moses dispatches twelve spies—one from each of the twelve tribes—to scout the land. The majority report from the spies is that, while the land itself is ideal for farming—"it flows with milk and honey" (Num 13:27)—its inhabitants are so big and strong that the spies believe them to be Nephilim (the giant demigods from chapter 2) and there is no way they can take the land. Because of their lack of trust, YHWH vows that no one from the generation of people that They rescued from slavery in Egypt will enter the land promised to their ancestors (save for Caleb and Joshua—the lone dissenters from the majority scouting report). The people are thus cursed to wander the Sinai Peninsula between Egypt and Canaan for the next forty years.

Sometimes the Hebrews' wilderness wandering is depicted as being lost in the desert, like a tourist with a broken GPS. But that's not how it was. According to Google Maps, you could walk from the Sinai Peninsula to Jerusalem in just over four days. Indeed, they had already made it to the border of the promised land. The Hebrews didn't spend forty years looking for a place just over the next ridge that they had already been to. They were following YHWH's glory.

Remember how, after the construction of the tabernacle, the dark cloud of YHWH's glory filled the tent so thick that even Moses wasn't able to enter? Well, from time to time, and it seems without warning, the cloud (or a great fire if it happened to be nighttime) would rise out of the tabernacle and waft somewhere across the peninsula. When it did, the Hebrews would hurriedly pack up the entire structure and follow. When the great cloud or fire came finally to alight elsewhere, they would carefully reconstruct the tabernacle to its exact specifications and wait for YHWH's glory to resume its position in the inner sanctum. YHWH's glory always appears in the form of things that cannot be firmly grasped—fire, cloud, smoke, or light. Here, the same idea is being communicated in a different way: YHWH's glory is mobile. You can't tie it down or predict where it will show up next. YHWH is a god on the move.

A MOBILE COSMIC MOUNTAIN

The layout of the tabernacle is theologically significant. Were you to happen upon it, you would first see a large fence made of twisted linen hanging from bronze pillars. This fence contains an area fifty cubits wide by a hundred cubits long. A cubit is notoriously difficult to convert since, depending on the text you're consulting, it is said to measure either the forearm (from the elbow to the tip of the middle finger) or six handbreadths (fingers not outstretched). But from best estimates, the court was probably about thirteen thousand square feet—approximately the size of an Olympic swimming pool.[1]

If you are a Hebrew, you are permitted to enter through the needlework-embroidered gate, into the courtyard of the tabernacle. There you see the altar on which animal sacrifices are made and a large bronze water basin used by priests for ritual washing. But you can't advance further. Only the priests can enter the tabernacle proper, called the holy place.

Inside the holy place stand two small tables holding incense, golden bowls for drink offerings, and a plate with twelve cakes of unleavened bread known as "the bread of the faces" (sometimes translated "showbread"). The priests bake a fresh batch every week and place it on the table for the Sabbath, so that YHWH has fresh bread before Them continually. Opposite the bread table is the menorah—a large lampstand constructed of pure gold with seven arms jutting out like the branches of a tree, and covered in decorative gold cups designed to look like the flowers of the almond tree. The menorah burns pure olive oil and is never to be extinguished.

Just behind the altar of incense hangs another curtain, similar to the one at the entrance to the court but with the addition of golden embroidered

---

1. See the discussion on cubits in Powell, "Weights and Measures," 897–908.

cherubim, sphinx-like divine beings who guard the boundary of Eden. This curtain is the entrance to the most holy place, or the holy of holies. Only the high priest is permitted entrance to the holy of holies, and only once a year, on the sacred day of *Yom Kippur* (the Day of Atonement).

Inside this small inner sanctum is the ark of the covenant—an acacia wood chest, gilded inside and out, with two long poles affixed to it by golden rings, so that it can be carried without being touched. The ark of the covenant holds the tablets on which Moses received the ten commandments; a pot of the manna with which YHWH fed the Hebrews in the wilderness; and Aaron's walking staff, by which it was revealed that Aaron's tribe—the Levites—would serve the tabernacle as its priests. The cover of the chest (called the "mercy seat") is made of pure gold and adorned with two golden statues of cherubim. Each cherub is bowing down to face the ark itself, their wings meet in the middle, giving the ark the shape of a chair with a backrest. For indeed, the ark of the covenant is YHWH's throne. Each time the Hebrews reassemble the tabernacle after a move, it is on the ark of the covenant—the mercy seat—that YHWH's glory rests.

Every detail of this ornate pattern is specifically designed to recapitulate prior mountaintop encounters with YHWH. Remember when YHWH's glory descended with trumpet blasts upon Mount Sinai as a great dark cloud? Mount Sinai was, at that moment, to the Hebrew conception at least, the center of the world. All the nations of the world were drawn around it. The Hebrews gathered around the foot of the mountain, but even they were not allowed to touch or approach the mountain itself, lest YHWH's glory break out and incinerate them. Aaron, his sons, and the seventy elders were able to ascend the mountain and gather around YHWH's footstool (outside the "throne room," as it were, atop the mountain). Only Moses was permitted entry into the throne room itself, in the dark cloud at the mountain's peak.

The tabernacle is modeled on this structure of tiered-access. Its fence marks the boundary of the nations, who are nevertheless drawn toward its center of gravity and nourished by its life-giving energy. The court of the tabernacle is the place where the Hebrew people gather around, as it were, the foothills of the divine palace. The priests maintain and care for the holy place just outside YHWH's throne room, just as Aaron and the elders ascended halfway up Mount Sinai to prepare the covenant ritual meal. There the priests encounter the arboreal menorah, representative of the plant life atop other cosmic mountains: the tree of life at the peak of Mount Eden, the thicket in which the life-giving ram was caught on Moriah, and the burning bush in which Moses encountered YHWH's glory on Sinai. And just as only Moses was granted entry into the dark cloud where he met with YHWH to receive the Torah, so only the high priest is permitted entry into the holy of holies to ritually cleanse YHWH's throne room. This is what the writer of the New Testament book of Hebrews meant when she said the tabernacle was "a sketch and shadow of the heavenly [sanctuary]" (Heb 8:5). The tabernacle was a mobile cosmic mountain.

ETHNIC CLEANSING

YHWH's presence is mobile so that Their people can follow it, first around the Sinai Peninsula, and then finally into the land They promised to Abraham. After forty years of wandering, Joshua—Moses' successor—leads the people into the land, where they conquer the indigenous population. The Bible describes this invasion in unnerving language:

> When the LORD your God brings you into the land that you are about to enter and occupy and he clears away many nations before you . . . and when the LORD your God gives them over to you and you defeat them, then you must utterly destroy them. Make no covenant with them and show them no mercy. . . . [B]reak down their altars, smash their pillars, cut down their sacred poles, and burn their idols with fire. For you are a people holy to the LORD your God; the LORD our God has chosen you out of all the peoples on earth to be his people, his treasured possession. (Deut 7:1–2, 5–6)

Modern ears cannot help but hear this description as commanding ethnic cleansing. Why would a god of love and peace demand such genocidal violence? Theologians and historians have taken a variety of approaches to deal with this contradiction in values.

Some have sought to justify the violence. Perhaps, it is suggested, these tribes were guilty of some crime or impurity—idolatry, human sacrifice, and descent from the Nephilim are all commonly invoked. Crafting such justifications for ethnic cleansing is a morally fraught exercise. There is no justification for genocide. Others, particularly historical-critical scholars, will often note that such an invasion and conquest almost certainly never occurred. Historically, this is a great relief. Nevertheless, within a narrative reading, it does little to resolve the problem. Even if fictionalized, we still have to explain why these authors would portray YHWH as giving such a heinous order.

Unfortunately, we cannot offer a satisfactory resolution to this tension. Perhaps no one can. In part, of course, this text (and others like it) reflect cultural and ethical norms from a historical period radically different from our own. If you read Homer's *Iliad*, Dante's *Divine Comedy*, or *Sir Gawain and the Green Knight*, you will find similarly strange and upsetting moments. We should not be surprised to find them in the biblical narrative as well. Nevertheless, unless we affirm a radical moral relativism, the tension remains. Perhaps we could point to the literary role of such texts. They are political propaganda, designed to elevate the glory and might of the Israelite kingdoms. But this solution is equally unsatisfying. Like the former, it doesn't address the central tension; it dodges it.

And so, rather than offering a resolution to this problem, we'd like to propose it as a place of reflection. We can turn away from such texts—by justifying them, tossing them into the dustbin of history, or (as is most common) ignoring them. Or, we can take them as an invitation to face the violence that lives at the heart of this story and at the heart of the world. The Bible is a living text. It continues to shape our world. If we ignore the genocide of the Amalekites in the biblical story, then we will be unprepared to respond to the invocation of the Amalekites to justify ongoing ethnic cleansing in our time. In 2023, amid the Israeli-Hamas war and ethnic cleansing of Gaza, Israeli Prime Minister Benjamin Netanyahu declared: "you must remember what Amalek has done to you, says our Holy Bible. And we do remember."[2] For those attuned to the biblical narrative, these words are horrifying. For, this is what YHWH commands of the king of Israel in the narrative:

> Thus says the LORD of hosts: I will punish the Amalekites for what they did in opposing the Israelites when they came up out of Egypt. Now go and attack Amalek and utterly destroy all that they have; do not spare them, but kill both man and woman, child and infant, ox and sheep, camel and donkey. (1 Sam 15:2–3)

Facing the violence within the biblical text better prepares us to face it when it reemerges in the contemporary world.

---

2. Lanard, "Dangerous History Behind Netanyahu's Amalek Rhetoric."

A KING LIKE THE OTHER NATIONS

The Hebrews first dwelled in the promised land of Canaan as a loose federation of tribes—twelve of them plus the Levites, a special tribe from whom the priests were called. The federation was governed by a series of theocratically appointed warrior chieftains, called judges. But social and political stability proved elusive, the tribes forever warring both with their neighbors and amongst themselves.

In response to the violence and disunity, the people demand that the final judge, Samuel, anoint a king to rule the tribes. Samuel tries to dissuade them; this level of power is dangerous. A king will conscript their sons into military service, levy taxes, and indenture slaves to maintain his military-royal complex. By demanding a king, Samuel insists, they are functionally asking to return to pharaoh's Egypt. But the people do not heed Samuel's warnings. They want a king, they say, "so that we also may be like other nations and that our king may govern us and go out before us and fight our battles" (1 Sam 8:20). They have completely missed the point. They have been called to be a "holy nation" (Exod 19:6)—precisely set apart as *different* from the other nations. Worse still, YHWH is to be the one "who goes before you . . . [and] who will fight for you" (Deut 1:30). In demanding a king, they have lost the plot entirely.

Nevertheless, YHWH relents and instructs Samuel to give the people what they ask for. If they want to make a bad decision, YHWH will afford them that freedom. The first king that Samuel anoints is Saul, the heir of a wealthy Benjamite donkey herdsman. Saul is everything people look for in a king. He's tall, handsome, and smart. He proves to be both a good leader and a talented military tactician. But the cracks start to show almost immediately.

War breaks out when Jonathan, Saul's son and general, undertakes an ill-advised attack on a military garrison in neighboring Philistia. When they see the Philistine army approaching with "thirty thousand chariots, and six thousand horsemen, and troops like the sand on the seashore in multitude" (1 Sam 13:5), the Israelites scatter like cockroaches. They hide in caves, wells, and tombs.

When King Saul sees his makeshift army deserting him, he calls for animals to be brought to him so that he might make a burnt offering, right where he stands on a military base. Here there is neither tabernacle nor priests; there is no incense, washing, or ritual. Saul usurps the priestly role in an attempt to force the hand of YHWH. Like the builders of the Tower of

Babel, Saul chooses coercive power over co-creative participation. He tries to seize control of the manifestation of YHWH—to make YHWH appear on his own terms.

But YHWH refuses to be constrained. YHWH abandons Saul and orders the prophet Samuel to secretly anoint a young shepherd named David as the new king. In an ironic plot twist, the increasingly troubled and depressed Saul even hires the musically talented David to ease his troubled mind—unaware that David has been anointed as his successor.

But David's skills extend beyond the harp. He quickly rises through the military ranks, after single-handedly defeating the giant Goliath (who, according to some traditions, was one of the few living remnants of the sons of god's rebellion at Hermon). As David's military prominence grows, so too does his celebrity. Soon, his popularity outstrips that of King Saul, as illustrated by the popular rallying cry "Saul has killed his thousands and David his ten thousands" (1 Sam 18:7).

Saul does not take well to this popular rejection. He becomes increasingly unhinged, lashing out violently at David—who remains in his employ as a court musician—hurling a spear at him while he plays the harp. The kingship of Israel has become fully dysfunctional, as both YHWH and Samuel had warned.

AN UNWANTED PALACE

After Saul dies in battle, David ascends the throne as the second king of Israel. Despite his own mistakes—and they are many and grievous (including sexual violence and murder)—David is nonetheless celebrated as a man after YHWH's own heart (1 Sam 13:14). Among David's first acts as king is to relocate the capital city to Jerusalem, where he builds himself a resplendent palace on the lower eastern hill. It is a bit embarrassing though—the king living in such ostentatious digs while YHWH camps outside in a tent. So David resolves to build YHWH a temple on Mount Zion.

Just as when the people demanded a king, YHWH is not thrilled by the idea of a temple. Have I ever asked, "Why have you not built me a house of cedar?" (2 Sam 7:7), They rhetorically demand. YHWH likes being mobile, moving among the people. Huge fancy buildings are for the kings and their obsession with power—not for YHWH. Like a permissive parent, YHWH eventually gives in to David's questionable idea. But while YHWH does allow David to *design* a temple for Mount Zion, They do not allow him to *build* the temple. David is a war-time king; his hands are stained with blood. The hands of death cannot build a temple for the god of life. But YHWH gives a promise: David's son Solomon will rule in peacetime. He will build YHWH's temple.

As promised, Solomon's reign is marked by peace and prosperity. Israel becomes a wealthy, powerful, and influential nation in the Levant. But the crown jewel of Solomon's reign is, without question, the construction of the temple on Mount Zion.

Like the tabernacle, the temple on Mount Zion is designed with three levels of increasing holiness and correspondingly selective purity clearance. The exterior court is where YHWH's people gather to worship and offer sacrifices. The holy place is where priests tend the fire of the menorah and the bread of the faces. The holy of holies is where even the high priest can enter only on the Day of Atonement. And like the tabernacle, the temple is marked with distinctively Edenic imagery: the menorah functions as a tree of life, the holy place is guarded by two towering Cherubim statues—evoking the guardians of the gate into Eden—and at the center of it all sits the ark of the covenant, the seat of YHWH's glory.

All the people of Israel gather for the grand opening of the temple. Solomon has invited all of the elders, heads of tribes, and other important political players to participate in the ceremony. Together they offer sacrifices to YHWH. "So many sheep and oxen" are sacrificed, we are told, "that they could not be counted or numbered" (1 Kgs 8:5). The priests carry all the sacred objects from the tent and place them meticulously in the new temple. Finally, they carry the ark of the covenant—YHWH's throne—into the holy of holies. Just as they set it down "a cloud filled the house of the LORD, so that the priests could not stand to minister because of the cloud, for the glory of the LORD filled the house of the LORD" (1 Kgs 8:10–11).

With the construction of the temple, the covenant blessings promised to Abraham have finally come to fruition. Abraham's family dwells in the land promised to him, where he himself was only a nomad. They are governed and protected by an anointed king. And YHWH dwells at last on the holy mountain. Things are looking good.

But looks can be deceiving.

THE FALL OF THE UNITED MONARCHY

Precisely at the moment when the covenant promises are fulfilled, the writers of the Tanakh weave unsettling details into the narrative. An ambivalent darkness haunts the proceedings of the monarchy. Like the opening scenes of a horror movie, the reader can feel in the pit of their stomach that something is not quite right.

Already in the reign of David—a man, supposedly, after YHWH's own heart—we find astounding levels of deceit, lust, and violence. While he should be leading his people, David instead luxuriates in his palace, using his royal power to compel Bathsheba, one of his subjects, to sleep with him. When he finds out Bathsheba is pregnant, he first tries to deceive her husband, Uriah, before ultimately arranging his murder in order to cover up the scandal.

Nor is Solomon's reign blameless. The book of Deuteronomy includes a code of kingly conduct. It reads, in part:

> [The king] must not acquire many horses for himself or return the people to Egypt in order to acquire more horses, since the LORD has said to you, "You must never return that way again." And he must not acquire many wives for himself or else his heart will turn away; also silver and gold he must not acquire in great quantity for himself. (Deut 17:16–17)

Compare this to Solomon's reign. Solomon secures "peace" through violence, turning a priestly nation into a military state. He assembles a massive army of chariots—pulled by horses, which, we are explicitly told, he gets *from Egypt* (the biblical texts aren't always subtle). He enters into numerous political marriages and joins his wives in their worship of other gods, even inside the temple itself. He acquires an unprecedented fortune, building himself a palace that dwarfs even his father's and which includes such ostentatious elements as twelve golden lions flanking the steps up to his throne.

The next king, Rehoboam, inherits all of his ancestors' vices and none of their virtues. He is violent, arrogant, and crude. He mocks his father's genitals while threatening increased brutality against Israel's slaves: "My little finger is thicker than my father's loins. . . . [M]y father laid on you a heavy yoke, I will add to your yoke. My father disciplined you with whips, but I will discipline you with scorpions" (1 Kgs 12:10–11). The result of Rehoboam's cruelty is as tragic as it is inevitable: the ten northernmost tribes secede and the once-united kingdom descends into civil war. In less than three generations, the supposed glory of the monarchy has torn the holy nation to shreds. The priestly kingdom has been infected with the destructive spirit of Babylon. "Like other nations," indeed!

In the South, Rehoboam maintains the capital city of Jerusalem and the temple on Mount Zion. His counterpart and rival, Jeroboam, governs the newly formed northern nation of Israel from Shechem, in the modern-day Palestinian city of Nablus, in the Israeli-occupied West Bank.

Worried that his people were in danger while making the journey to Jerusalem to offer sacrifices in the temple, Jeroboam erects two statues of YHWH in the form of golden calves—one in Bethel, the southernmost city of his kingdom, and the other in the north at Dan. In the desert, YHWH was a god on the move, dwelling in a makeshift mobile tent, which Their people would pack up at a moment's notice to follow the cloud. But once the royal idea of confining YHWH's presence to a permanent temple took root, kings began to delude themselves that they could control the manifestation of YHWH's glory. Now the Hebrew people approach YHWH on their own terms at one of three convenient locations.

Eventually, worship in the northern kingdom of Israel will become centralized on Mount Gerizim, in Shechem, where another temple is constructed to rival the one on Mount Zion. Gerizim vs. Zion: rival cosmic temple mountains—each symbolizing an attempt to control the divine manifestation.

In the Gospel of John in the New Testament, Jesus will meet a woman who is a descendant of the northern Kingdom of Israel at a well near Mount Gerizim. Realizing that Jesus is a prophet, she confronts him about what she assumes to be their most important theological disagreement: "Our ancestors worshiped on this mountain, but you say that the place where people must worship is in Jerusalem" (John 4:20). Reigniting the vision of the tabernacle, Jesus prophesies that a day will come when the worship of YHWH will not be contained on either mountain and YHWH's justice will once again dwell among the people.

6

Horeb
The Mountain of Sacred Silence

MOUNT HOREB APPEARS TO suffer from an identity crisis. Throughout the biblical text, this single mountain goes by two names: Horeb and Sinai—yes, *that* Sinai. Are these two names for the same mountain? Two nearby mountains? Is one the name of a mountain range, and the other a prominent peak within that range? A medieval Jewish philosopher, Abraham ibn Ezra, even suggested that it was perhaps one mountain with two peaks. While a unanimous consensus has evaded scholars, the dominant interpretation points to Horeb and Sinai being two names for the same mountain, perhaps names emerging in different times or contexts. For this reason, we face the same difficulty pinning down the site of Horeb as we did with Sinai (see chapter 4). Nevertheless, Christian tradition has held that Mount Horeb was located at Ras es-Safsafeh, a peak adjacent to the traditional site of Mount Sinai (Jabal Musa). The conjunction of these two peaks was marked by Saint Catherine's Monastery, the oldest continually inhabited monastery in the world. Built on the supposed site of the burning bush, this ancient monastery contains the oldest running library in the world, containing a collection of early texts and codices second only to the Vatican library in Rome—including the *Codex Sinaiticus*, one of the earliest near-complete copies of the Christian Bible.

In the wilderness of the Sinai Peninsula, a weary prophet of YHWH rests in the cave at the top of this mountain. Elijah is lost, starving, and depressed. In a moment of hangry suicidal ideation, he begs YHWH to kill him: "It is enough; now, YHWH, take away my life" (1 Kgs 19:4). Alone on the mountaintop, chased from his home by a corrupt king, the depressed prophet seeks any experience of the divine, even if it is a deadly one.

It is no coincidence that Elijah chooses to seek YHWH on Mount Horeb. It was before this very mountain that the Israelites gathered in the desert. It was on this mountain that YHWH appeared in fire and storm. It was on this mountain that YHWH gifted Moses the tablets of the Torah and the blueprint for the tabernacle, as the people renewed their covenant. And so, in his moment of crisis, Elijah returns to this mountain of promise to listen for the voice of YHWH.

After giving Elijah a much-needed snack, an angel instructs him to go out to the entrance of the cave and await a manifestation of YHWH. From there, Elijah watches a blistering wind tear across the mountains with such intensity that it breaks rocks into pieces. Someone less sensitively attuned than a prophet like Elijah might have assumed this was just the manifestation the angel had foretold. But YHWH is not in the wind.

Soon the mountain itself begins to shake with a tremendous earthquake. But YHWH is not in the earthquake. After the earthquake, the mountain erupts in fire. But YHWH is not in the fire. Finally, Elijah hears a quiet sound, barely a whisper—translated in the King James Version as "a still small voice"—but it could perhaps equally well be translated, "the sound of sheer silence." In the silence, Elijah perceives a question: "What are you doing here?"

This is not the glorious manifestation of YHWH that Elijah was expecting on Mount Horeb. It is not the fire in the storm. It is not the magnificent divine glory. Rather, Elijah is among the first in the biblical text to face YHWH's silence. For, unbeknownst to Elijah, a greater crisis is fast approaching. Injustice and idolatry have spread among YHWH's covenant partners, and they are about to be called to account.

THE RISE OF THE PROPHETS

The crisis that drove Elijah to Horeb began a couple hundred miles to the north on another mountain, in the northern kingdom of Israel—Mount Carmel. At this time, the northern Kingdom of Israel was ruled by King Ahab. Like many rulers in this critical period, Ahab failed in his task to lead his people, both spiritually and politically. Together with the worship of YHWH, the northern kingdom had a well-developed cult of Baal, a Canaanite deity.

It was in the midst of the violence and idolatry of King Ahab and the other rulers of the northern kingdom of Israel and the southern kingdom of Judah that YHWH's spirit empowered a group of exemplary figures to speak out. Preaching the fiery words of YHWH, these prophets condemned the kingdoms for their failure to uphold the covenant and bring a blessing to all the nations.

Today, many people hear the word "prophet" and imagine a fortune-teller hunched over a crystal ball predicting the future. But the prophets of the Hebrew Scriptures are not fortune-tellers. While it is undoubtedly true that the prophets, like fortune-tellers, often speak of the future, they speak with a different grammar than fortune-tellers do.

When you call the fortune-teller on their 1–800 number, they speak to you in the future tense: "you *will* meet the love of your life this week"; "you *will* get a new job!"; "you *will* experience a tragic loss . . . ." The fortune-teller (purportedly) tells you what *will happen*.

The Hebrew prophets use a different grammar. They speak in the subjunctive mood. They employ an if/then structure: "*if* you continue to oppress the poor, *then* the nation will face judgment"; "*if* you worship other gods, *then* YHWH will turn against you." Prophets don't say what will happen *as such*. Rather, they inform their audience of what will happen *if* they don't change their ways. Prophets don't think in terms of fate; they think in terms of *consequences*. A prophet is like the orange sign in the middle of the road that says, "Bridge Out Ahead." Their goal is to get their audience to turn around, to change course, to shift their behavior and avoid the anticipated catastrophe. If the prophet does their job well, their prophecy will never come to pass.

Ironically, you can see this structure most clearly by looking at the *worst* prophet in the Hebrew Scriptures. Jonah is a prophet who refuses to preach the word of YHWH. Jonah is given a terrible burden. YHWH calls him to preach in Nineveh, the capital city of the Assyrian Empire, the very people who—spoiler alert—will destroy the entire northern kingdom of Israel. He is supposed to help the monsters who conquered his people avoid YHWH's judgment. Understandably, Jonah refuses. He takes the quickest route in the opposite direction from Nineveh. That is when, in the story famous from Sunday School classes and Children's Bibles, Jonah is thrown into the sea, swallowed by a giant fish, and spat back out onto dry land, so that he can complete his difficult prophetic task. Jonah capitulates with the reluctance of a teenager being forced to write a thank-you card to his Great Aunt Edna for the hand-knit Christmas sweater. He goes to Nineveh and delivers a pitiful five-word sermon. Yet, despite Jonah's lousy preaching and open disdain for his congregation, the Assyrians actually heed his message. They show genuine remorse and make real changes and are thereby saved from the coming disaster. Jonah is the most successful prophet in the Hebrew Scriptures, and it is entirely by accident. He is furious about it. He rage-prays to YHWH: "Is not this what I said while I was still in my own country? That is why I fled to Tarshish at the beginning; for I knew that you are a gracious God and merciful, slow to anger, and abounding in steadfast love, and ready to relent from punishing" (Jonah 4:2).

This is what it means to be a prophet: to preach the words of YHWH—even if reluctantly—so that there might be a genuine transformation, a turn in a new direction. The tragedy of the prophets is that Jonah is an outlier. With few exceptions, the prophets' warnings are ignored. Their audiences plow forward like nothing is wrong, even as the prophets warn of impending disaster. The nations of Judah and Israel barrel toward the missing bridge without a second thought. The results are catastrophic.

Because the prophets' warnings are so rarely taken seriously, one can find a consistent structure in prophetic stories. First, the prophet anticipates crisis, destruction, and judgment. Second, the people ignore the prophet's warnings and continue on their path. Third, destruction ensues—violence rains down upon the hard-hearted people as the pain and oppression that they inflicted on their most vulnerable neighbors ricochets back on them. Finally, there is a promise of restoration. For even if the prophetic warning is ignored, even if the nation drives full speed off the missing bridge, YHWH's covenant promises ultimate restoration. Remember how, when the covenant was ratified, the smoking fire pot passed through the sacrificed animals as Abraham slept soundly under a tree? YHWH will remain faithful even if his people do not. They may face unimaginably difficult trials, but YHWH's partnership with them remains in force. So the prophets anticipate a dawn after the darkest nights, new birth after the pangs of labor, a glimmer of hope, restoration, and return.

THE PROPHETIC CRITIQUE

The prophetic critique has two main targets. First, the prophets attack idolatry and religious infidelity. The prophets of Israel are the world's first strict monotheists. YHWH is the only god who should be worshiped by the Hebrew people, they say—no exceptions. This is a bold claim at a time when religious syncretism (the mixing of beliefs and practices from multiple religious traditions) was common among the average Judean or Israelite.

Second, the prophets critique social injustice. Particularly, they are infuriated by injustice perpetrated against the most vulnerable members of society. These vulnerable people are emblematized and epitomized by four figures known in modern scholarship as "the quartet of the vulnerables"—the poor, the immigrant, the orphan, and the widow. Each of these four figures represents how one might find oneself without access to the basic means of survival. They depend upon justice and mercy for their very life. To be poor in the ancient world was to be without access to land and harvest; to be an immigrant was to be without the safety net of the community; to be an orphan or a widow was to lack the male head-of-household, the primary breadwinner in a patriarchal society. The prophet Zechariah put it succinctly: "Do not oppress the widow, the orphan, the alien, or the poor; and do not devise evil in your hearts against one another" (Zech 7:4). Concern for these vulnerable members of the community required (and still requires) an expansive view of our responsibility to the other, whether our neighbor or a foreign stranger.

The prophets do not see idolatry and injustice as two distinct and unrelated concerns. The prophets are not worried about religion on the one hand and politics or economics on the other. They understand these as two sides of a single coin. On their logic, if you properly worship YHWH, the god of justice and mercy, then YHWH's justice and mercy will be reflected in your care for the most vulnerable members of your community. Conversely, if you don't show concern for the most vulnerable members of your community, then it doesn't matter what name you say when you pray, you don't *really* worship YHWH. For these prophets, right worship leads to just action and just action reveals right worship. There is no room in the prophetic paradigm for the banker who spends Monday through Friday bankrupting the poor and evicting the needy and then goes to church on Sunday to sing a few songs and say a few prayers. As the prophet Amos says, in the voice of YHWH and with startling directness:

> I hate, I despise your festivals,
>   and I take no delight in your solemn assemblies.
> Even though you offer me your burnt offerings and grain offerings,
>   I will not accept them,
> and the offerings of well-being of your fatted animals
>   I will not look upon.
> Take away from me the noise of your songs;
>   I will not listen to the melody of your harps.
> But let justice roll down like water
>   and righteousness like an ever-flowing stream. (Amos 5:21–24)

If we don't care for the vulnerable members of our society, YHWH stops listening to our prayers. That's prophecy in the Hebrew tradition.

The Hebrew prophets radically transformed ethics and politics, gauging the health of their society by looking to the vulnerable, rather than the rich and the powerful. By this measure, both the northern kingdom of Israel and the southern kingdom of Judah were found wanting. The prophet Amos, for example, experiences a vision of a plumb line (Amos 7) being held up against a great wall. (A plumb line is like a level, except it tells you if a wall is straight in the vertical direction.) The result is not good. The wall is determined to be irredeemably crooked. YHWH informs Amos that it must be torn down to its foundation and rebuilt from scratch. The message is not subtle. It is bad news for the two kingdoms.

A PROPHETS' DUEL

Elijah (whom we left at the top of Mount Horeb) is given this difficult prophetic task. He must speak on behalf of YHWH—a voice crying out in the wilderness, demanding justice for the poor and the oppressed and re-orienting the religious values of his community. Such audacity will bring Elijah into direct confrontation with King Ahab—a king who not only permitted the worship of Baal, but built a temple to Baal in Israel.

If YHWH has Elijah, so too does Baal have prophets. And so, on the top of another mountain—Mount Carmel—Elijah challenges these prophets of Baal to a wizard's duel worthy of J. R. R. Tolkien's pen. Elijah himself sets the rules of the engagement. Each side will assemble an altar and place upon it the meat of a butchered bull. They will then pray to their respective gods, asking for fire to rain down from the heavens and consume the offering. The prophets whose offering is consumed will be victorious; their god will be proven true. The stakes of the bet will be the prophets' lives.

The prophets of Baal go first. They select their bull, butcher it, and place it on the altar. They cry out to Baal from morning until noon. But there is no answer and no fire. Elijah mocks them: "Cry aloud! Surely he is a god; either he is meditating, or he has wandered away, or he is on a journey, or perhaps he is asleep and must be awakened" (1 Kgs 18:27). And so the prophets cry out louder; they begin ritually cutting themselves with swords and sprinkling their blood around the altar. All this to no avail. Their sacrifice remains on the altar, unscorched.

Elijah's turn is next. He builds an altar for YHWH, assembling twelve stones—one for each of the tribes of Israel. He prepares the wood and the bull, placing them on the altar. Then, in an ostentatious display of confidence, Elijah instructs his assistants to douse the altar with water, not once or twice but three times. By the time they finish, the water runs down the altar and fills a trench around it. Only when the altar is thoroughly soaked through does Elijah begin to pray: "O LORD, God of Abraham, Isaac, and Israel, let it be known this day that you are God in Israel, that I am your servant, and that I have done all these things at your bidding. Answer me, O LORD, answer me, so that this people may know that you, O LORD, are God and that you have turned their hearts back" (1 Kgs 18:36–37). All of a sudden, the fire of YHWH erupts from the sky and consumes the burnt offering, the wood, even the twelve stones. As soon as they see the fire descend, onlookers begin falling to the ground to worship YHWH. Elijah commands his assistants to seize the prophets of Baal, bring them down to a stream, and publicly execute them.

When King Ahab tells his queen, Jezebel, what Elijah has done—how at the culmination of the duel he executed the prophets of Baal—Jezebel is enraged. Immediately, she demands Elijah's life. It's at this point that Elijah flees into the wilderness of Mount Horeb, where he prays for a theophany but experiences the sound of silence.

Elijah would not be the last prophet to face a royal rage. As the spokespeople of YHWH—demanding costly justice from the rich and powerful—prophets had an extremely dangerous job. It is for this reason that, by the time of Jesus, eight centuries later, tradition held that the prophets were almost uniformly murdered by their own people. As Jesus proclaims to the Judeans of his time, "you are descendants of those who murdered the prophets. . . . Jerusalem, Jerusalem, the city that kills the prophets and stones those who are sent to it!" (Matt 23:31, 37).

Surprisingly, this would not be Elijah's fate. He would instead join his ancestor Enoch (whom we met in chapter 2) in bypassing death entirely. Passing the mantle of prophet to his most trusted student, Elisha, Elijah ascends directly to the heavenly throne room on a fiery chariot. There, according to a later prophet, Malachi, he awaits the day of YHWH's ultimate judgment; "See, I will send you the prophet Elijah before the great and terrible day of the LORD comes" (Mal 4:5).

THE DAY OF YHWH

This day that the now heaven-dwelling Elijah anticipates is a central theme of the Hebrew prophets' message. Its name—the Day of YHWH—is rooted in the Passover event in the book of Exodus. On that day, YHWH liberated his people from the slavery and oppression of the Egyptians.

By Malachi's time, political circumstances had deteriorated such that a popular idea began to emerge that another day was coming, a day even greater than the Passover. This ultimate Day of YHWH began to crystallize into an eschatological vision of the liberation of the covenant people. In the Jewish imagination, the Day of YHWH is the day when all things will be set right: oppressive empires will be cast into the sea and Israel will be set as the greatest among the nations. This day became so central to Hebrew self-identity that soon it would be referred to simply as "the Day." There are days, and then there is *the Day*. One can see how, in this royal theology of the Day of YHWH, demands for genuine justice sit together uncomfortably with nascent nationalism.

At the same time, however, there is another vision of the Day of the YHWH—that of the prophets. Amos, one of the first Hebrew prophets, exemplifies this alternate viewpoint when he declares:

> Woe to you who desire the day of the LORD!
>   Why do you want the day of the LORD?
> It is darkness, not light,
>   as if someone fled from a lion
>   and was met by a bear
>   or went into the house and rested a hand against the wall
>   and was bitten by a snake.
> Is not the day of the LORD darkness, not light,

and gloom with no brightness in it? (Amos 5:18–20)

For Amos, the Day of YHWH is the day when the oppressed will be raised up and their unrighteous oppressors will be struck down. This is wonderful news if you are oppressed. But if YHWH's people have become unrighteous, if they no longer treat one another with justice and mercy—if, in short, they have become the oppressors—then this is very bad news. They should not look forward to the day of YHWH. They should fear it, as should everyone who fails to uphold the justice of YHWH. What had, in the hands of the rich and the powerful, been a nationalistic anticipation of ultimate victory; became, in the hands of the prophets, a dire warning. For the prophets, no one, no matter how rich or powerful, can escape ultimate justice.

Amid the violence and injustice of their time, the prophets begin to anticipate a coming catastrophe. They look at the world around them and see that ruin is inevitable. They offer countless warnings to the political, economic, and religious authorities but their warnings are ignored. And so the crisis comes.

THE CRISIS OF EXILE

In 722 BCE, the Neo-Assyrian Empire invades and conquers the northern kingdom of Israel. The ten northern tribes of the Hebrews are swept away in an instant and ultimately will be lost to history. The southern kingdom of Judah hardly fares better. In 588 BCE, Nebuchadnezzar II, the king of the Neo-Babylonian Empire, leads a similar campaign against Judah. He destroys the capital of Jerusalem and—after stripping it of gold and fine jewels—burns the temple of YHWH to the ground. He then marches the survivors to captivity in Babylon. These events are an exact inversion of the Day of YHWH as it was anticipated in royal theology. But they are precisely the catastrophe the prophets had warned about. The destructive spirit of Babylon has come with chariot and sword.

It is hard to overestimate the depth of this trauma—socially, politically, and religiously. How could YHWH allow the covenant people to be enslaved again? How could They allow the lineage of the Davidic dynasty to be cut off? How could They allow Their own temple to be burned to the ground? Was YHWH immolated in the fire?

From the Babylonian perspective, this conquest is undoubtedly interpreted as the victory of their pantheon over the god of Israel. As on earth the Babylonian forces demolish the temple of YHWH, so in the heavens Marduk, the chief Babylonian deity, overcomes YHWH.

The prophet Ezekiel offers a different, but in some ways no less theologically disturbing, interpretation of this event. Ezekiel is among the first group of exiles, already living in Babylon at the time of the final assault on the city of Jerusalem. From his place of exile, he preaches a theological interpretation of the crisis unfolding back home. He insists that YHWH was not defeated by the forces of Babylon. Instead, he suggests, employing traditional prophetic logic, YHWH has used Babylon and its chaotic violence to exact justice against the covenant people. Babylon is nothing more than a pawn in the chess match of which YHWH plays both sides.

Ezekiel's vision might seem comforting, as no doubt he intended it to be. But this theological interpretation has a dark side, too. To make his case, Ezekiel reports a mystical vision he was given. In Ezekiel's dream, as the Babylonian forces breach the walls of Jerusalem and begin to destroy the city, YHWH, in the holy of holies at the center of the temple, mounts a flaming chariot and departs into the clouds. According to Ezekiel, in the moment of greatest crisis, YHWH abandons the covenant people.

DEAFENING SILENCE

In the excruciating loneliness of exile, the Hebrews compose songs of mourning.

> By the rivers of Babylon—
>   there we sat down, and there we wept
>   when we remembered Zion.
> On the willows there
>   we hung up our harps.
> For there our captors
>   asked us for songs,
> and our tormentors asked for mirth, saying,
>   "Sing us one of the songs of Zion!" (Ps 137:1–3)

Poetry in a time of loss is a cry of rage. This same melancholic psalm ends with the startlingly honest expression of unmitigated fury:

> O daughter Babylon, you devastator!
>   Happy shall they be who pay you back
>   what you have done to us!
> Happy shall they be who take your little ones

and dash them against the rock! (Ps 137:8–9)

It is in this way that the Hebrew Scriptures come to a close. They end neither in triumphant victory nor in apocalyptic catastrophe, but in the quiet, traumatic aftermath of a great loss. In the periods following the Babylonian exile, many of the Judeans would eventually be permitted to return to their homeland. There they would rebuild the walls of Jerusalem. They would even begin to rebuild the temple. But the ten northern tribes, conquered by the Assyrians, would never return. And even for those southern tribes who could return, a nagging sense of exile and alienation will persist. Like Elijah on Mount Horeb, they will continue to look for signs. They will hope and pray for a miraculous manifestation of YHWH to appear in fire and glory and to set all things right. But what they will experience is sheer silence, the deafening nothing of exile.

7

Tabor
The Mountain of Unveiling

IN LOWER GALILEE, BETWEEN the Jezreel Valley and the Sea of Galilee, Mount Tabor rises suddenly from the level vineyards of the grape-farming village below. It was there that a woman named Jael—who was not a Hebrew but, according to the book of Judges, was married to a descendant of Moses' father-in-law—saved the Hebrew people from being overtaken by Canaan. She invited Sisera, the commander of the Canaanite armies, into her tent for some refreshments and a nap and then drove a tent peg through his skull while he slept. Today, a Roman Catholic church and a Greek Orthodox church stand on either side of the mountain overlooking the entirely Jewish town of Kfar Tavor.

In the midst of his short ministry, Jesus, an itinerant preacher from the backwater town of Nazareth, took three of his closest disciples for a hike up a mountain, which, according to a tradition dating back to at least the third century CE, was this Mount Tabor. By the time they had reached the summit, Jesus had been mystically transformed such that, "his face shone like the sun, and his clothes became bright as light" (Matt 17:2). Peter, one of these disciples, understands the profound significance of this moment. They are experiencing a theophany, a vision of YHWH. "Rabbi," he exclaims, "it is good for us to be here; let us set up three tents" (Matt 17:4). But can they dwell in the peak experience?

WHY DO THE OLD PEOPLE WEEP?

In the fall of 539 BCE, the Jews' captors, the Neo-Babylonian Empire, fell to King Cyrus the Great and the Achaemenid Empire at the Battle of Opis. Soon Cyrus would permit a number of Jews to return to Jerusalem and rebuild the ruins of their fallen capital.

Only the two southernmost tribes—which comprise the nation of Judah—were given this opportunity of return. The other ten of the original twelve tribes of the Hebrews were never subject to Cyrus' rule and were thus not beneficiaries of his offer. They had instead been carted off to Assyria, where they would assimilate with the local population until their Jewish identity was forever lost to history. Cyrus was willing for his subjects to return to the land of their ancestors only because there could be no pretense that the land belonged to them—it was decidedly Cyrus' land. The subsequent kings Judah would rarely be real kings, only the puppets of a series of foreign emperors. Still, after more than half a century in the silence of exile, many Jews would return to their homeland and, perhaps most importantly, rebuild YHWH's temple.

At the groundbreaking ceremony of this second temple, priests blew trumpets gathering throngs of congregants to celebrate the renewal of the covenant with YHWH. Ezra recounts the event:

> [The priests] sang responsively, praising and giving thanks to the LORD, "For he is good, for his steadfast love endures forever toward Israel." And all the people responded with a great shout when they praised the LORD because the foundation of the house of the LORD had been laid. But many of the priests and Levites and heads of families, old people who had seen the first house on its foundations, wept with a loud voice when they saw this house, though many shouted aloud for joy, so that the people could not distinguish the sound of the joyful shout from the sound of the people's weeping, for the people shouted so loudly that the sound was heard far away. (Ezra 3:11–13)

Why do the old people weep? They weep because they remember the story of the opening ceremony of the first temple—when YHWH's glory filled the house with such an overwhelming presence that the priests themselves could not stand in the holy place. But now, it seems, the glory has not returned. The priests are here in their vestments and with their trumpets, but there is no fire, no cloud, no smoke, no light. All the religious trappings of the temple are here . . . but YHWH is absent.

As a result, in the centuries following their return, Jewish prophets became increasingly convinced that YHWH's work in history was not done. In beautiful poetry and visionary images, they anticipated the true and full restoration of the covenant. For some Jews, these anticipations began to center upon a figure who stood for the intervention of YHWH into history: the messiah—an anointed warrior-king who would overthrow the occupying empire, restore the Davidic kingdom, and cleanse the temple in anticipation of the return of YHWH's glory.

THE REIGN OF YHWH

It is out of this social and political matrix that an itinerant preacher appears in the Roman-occupied Galilean countryside, proclaiming an imminent reign of YHWH—or, as it's often translated in the patriarchal idiom of the day, "the kingdom of God." He says: "The time is fulfilled, and the kingdom of God has come near; repent, and believe in the good news" (Mark 1:15). These are Jesus of Nazareth's first recorded words and he simply says, "It's time." What time is he announcing? He's announcing that the messianic time of the reign of YHWH is at hand. To Jesus' audience, this announcement would signal the return of YHWH to the land, the reclamation of YHWH's people, the renewal of YHWH's house—the temple—and the restoration of YHWH's representative to the Davidic throne.

But to those who have ears to hear, this announcement also has a radical religio-political edge. For there is already a temple in Jerusalem, though Ezra's old men may have perceived it to be devoid of glory. The temple is nevertheless administered by Jerusalem's social elite, a "burden" for which they are compensated handsomely. There are, moreover, at least three people who have some claim to the title king over the Jewish people: Pontius Pilate, the Roman governor of Judaea, which includes Jerusalem; Herod Antipas, the client tetrarch ruling over Galilee and Perea; and not least the Roman emperor, Tiberius himself. To speak of the renewal of the temple implies the obsolescence of the current one, and thus of the Judean ruling elite. The reclamation of the Davidic throne signals the ouster of current claimants to that throne. If YHWH is King, Caesar is not.

But Jesus does not only threaten the position of Tiberias, Pilate, Herod, and the Judean ruling class—as if that were not enough. For Jesus knows his history. Every Jew in the first century did. They watched it play out before their very eyes, they felt it in their bones. Rome is just the latest empire threatening to destroy YHWH's chosen people. From Egypt to Assyria, from Babylon to Persia and Greece, the history of the land of Palestine is one of occupation and resistance, even up to the present day. If Jesus' vision of a reign of YHWH is to be realized, the very spirit of Babylon must be overcome—the spiritual sickness that underlies every human empire and all human oppression. And so, Jesus' public activity as an itinerant faith healer, exorcist, and wisdom teacher takes aim, not at political leaders, but at evil, sin, and death—the principal weapons of the spirit of Babylon.

FAITH HEALER AND EXORCIST

Once, in Capernaum—the small fishing village on the northern shore of the Sea of Galilee that had become the home base of Jesus' activity—a group of friends came to see Jesus. Four of them carried a fifth on a mat. The latter had suffered some sort of paralysis that evidently left him unable to walk. After lumbering all the way in this manner, the friends saw that Jesus' teaching had drawn such a crowd that they couldn't even elbow their way into the door. The friends, nonplussed, climbed up onto the roof and started tearing the shingles off. Having dug all the way through the roof they lowered their friend down on his mat to the feet of Jesus.

Had Jesus continued to teach through all this commotion? It's hard to imagine. Either way, they certainly have his attention now. Seeing the loyalty of this man's friends, Jesus looks at him and says something unexpected. Jesus had earned a reputation around Capernaum as a faith healer. Doubtless, this is why the men had resorted to such drastic measures to get their friend to see him: they expected Jesus to heal their friend's paralysis. Instead, Jesus looks at the man and says, "Child, your sins are forgiven" (Mark 2:5).

Why would Jesus say this? It sounds insensitive at best. Surely he knew why these people trudged through the Galilean sun carrying their friend on their shoulders and defaced a stranger's home. Why is he changing the subject like this? But for Jesus, this isn't changing the subject. In the context of his announcement that the reign of YHWH has come near—the very thing he would have been speaking about in that house—this man's paralysis is not separable from the covenant people's failure to provide for the orphan, the widow, and the immigrant. Announcing one characteristic of the reign of YHWH—the forgiveness of sin—is tantamount to proclaiming the return of YHWH, the renewal and restructuring of the temple, and the replacement of the oppressive Roman occupation with YHWH's representative to the Davidic throne.

Jesus doesn't have to make all of this explicit. His audience understands his meaning intuitively. That's why the religious leaders among the crowd lash out. "It is blasphemy!" they shout. "Who can forgive sins but God alone?" (Mark 2:7). In other words, who does this person think he is, offering forgiveness of sins apart from the religious system we have constructed? Their livelihoods depend in part on the scarcity of this service, and here is Jesus giving it away for free.

It is at this point that Jesus heals the man's paralysis, so that the outraged religious authorities "may know that [he] has authority on earth to forgive sins" (Mark 2:10). He instructs the man to "stand up, take your mat, and go to your home" (Mark 2:11). And the man does just that.

Today, sociologists and theologians alike have come to understand disability, not as a medical condition from which an individual needs to be healed, but a social construction.[1] That is to say, disability is the result of the interaction between individuals with various physical and mental impairments and the physical and social infrastructure of their society, which tends to be designed to cater to the needs of typical bodies and in turn to create barriers to access for impaired bodies. We don't want to make Jesus into the consummate progressive by suggesting that he had a theory of disability two millennia ahead of its time, or otherwise rescue him from being bound by his particular place and perspective in history. But it is interesting that Jesus performs this miraculous healing as a point in an implicit argument about Jewish covenant renewal, in which personal and spiritual transformation are situated within the context of religious, social, and political restructuring.

Just as Jesus demonstrates his authority over spiritual realities by offering physical healing, he also demonstrates his victory over the powers of darkness by interacting with people who appear to be possessed by unclean spirits or demons. These demons are, according to some traditions, the spiritual residue of the defeated Nephilim—literal giant ghosts![2] In a

---

1. See, for instance, Oliver, *Politics of Disablement*; Eiesland, *Disabled God*.

2. The traditions that connects demons to the spirits of deceased Nephilim is most clearly articulated in *1 Enoch* and the book of *Jubilees*. In the latter, for example, we are introduced to the "impure demons" (10:1) and told that the watchers are "the fathers of these spirits" (10:5); i.e., they are Nephilim, the children of watcher fathers and human women (see chapter 2). YHWH initially condemns these spirits to an eternal prison. But, faced with a petition from Mastema, the leader of the unclean spirits, They partially

Capernaum synagogue (a community center and house of Torah study), Jesus is confronted by a man with unclean spirits. The supernatural beings who possess this man, defiant though they may be, seem to know things about Jesus' identity that his less spiritually attuned audience do not recognize. In a scene fit for *The Exorcist*, one of the spirits shrieks: "What have you to do with us, Jesus of Nazareth? Have you come to destroy us? I know who you are, the Holy One of God" (Mark 1:24). Jesus orders the demons to be quiet and to exit his host. The demons' departure isn't quiet, exactly. They literally go kicking and screaming, leaving their host convulsing and crying on the floor. But he says nothing more about who Jesus is.

THE MESSIANIC SECRET

It is a strange and interesting feature of this story that Jesus seems not to want the demon to reveal who he is. This is a common theme in the Gospel tradition, though. Particularly in Mark, stories of Jesus' encounters with the demon possessed often include the detail that "he would not permit the demons to speak, because they knew him" (Mark 1:34). He even swore a man to silence after healing his skin disease (Mark 1:40–45). That man was not as obedient as the demons and quickly spread the word across town.

Jesus resists being understood or defined. That seems also to be the reason he teaches about the reign of YHWH in enigmatic stories about farmers, gardeners, vineyards, and fig trees, which consistently baffle and confuse his audience. It is only his closest disciples to whom he gives the secret meanings of the parables (Mark 4:11).

It seems in keeping with this clandestine nature that, on their way to Caesarea Philippi (in what is now the Israeli-occupied Golan Heights

---

relent and permit 1/10th of the spirits to remain on the earth for the purpose of "destroying and misleading" (10:8). Nowhere does the New Testament explicitly articulate this position, but significant circumstantial evidence (for example, the descent of Jesus to the entombed unclean spirits, see 1 Pet 3:18–20) suggests that it was a popular view among early Christians.

As Michael Heiser remarks: "The New Testament is silent on the origin of demons. There is no passage that describes a primeval rebellion before Eden where angels fell from grace and became demons. The origin of demons in Jewish texts outside of the Bible (such as 1 Enoch) is attributed to the events of Genesis 6:1–4. When a Nephilim was killed in these texts, its disembodied spirit was considered a demon. These demons then roamed the earth to harass humans. The New Testament does not explicitly embrace this belief, though there are traces of the notion, such as demon possession of humans (implying the effort to be re-embodied)." Heiser, *Unseen Realm*, 325; cf. 99n16.

region of Syria), Jesus inquires of his disciples what people have been saying about him. He wants to know if word has gotten out. The disciples report the popular opinion that Jesus might be a reincarnation of one of the prophets, like Elijah or John the Baptizer. But then Jesus gets more direct: "But who do you say that I am?" (Mark 8:29). Mark places this stark and crucial question on the lips of his protagonist here, in the central passage of his Gospel, because it is the question on which the entire book hinges.

Having witnessed Jesus forgive sins by his own authority, overcome illness, impairment, and demonic spirits, and teach in bizarre and perplexing stories, it is becoming increasingly clear to his disciples that Jesus is positioning himself as the anointed king of the line of David; the one who will restore YHWH's reign. But it is Simon alone who first whispers the secret: "You are the messiah" (Mark 8:29). Jesus, of course, sternly orders him not to speak of it again.

All this secrecy makes perfect sense once one considers that the establishment of the reign of YHWH implies the deposition of the Roman occupation. A would-be rebel king could not have Pontius Pilate catching wind of insurrection before a plan was even hatched. Trained in his father's carpentry shop, Jesus understands that a builder must carefully consider all the costs before laying a foundation.

But there is one glaring problem with this plan. As we have seen, the coming reign of YHWH will not require *only* the overthrow of the Roman occupation. The whole purpose of reclaiming the Davidic throne from the occupying empire and renewing the temple is to prepare the way for *YHWH's return to Zion*. And nothing about YHWH's presence is circumspect or subtle. The last time YHWH entered the temple, the priests couldn't even stand in the holy place, so thick was the cloud of divine glory. If YHWH were to return to Zion, as Jesus' announcement seems to suggest, then surely the religious authorities—the very people whom Jesus has been so keen to keep in the dark about his identity and mission—would be the first to know. Yet soon the light of divine glory will shine, but not in Zion. Rather, the light shines on an insignificant mountain, out of view of the religious elites.

TRANSFIGURATION

It is not long after Simon Peter divulges Jesus' messianic ambitions that Jesus takes him, along with James and John, on the transformative hike up Mount Tabor. According to Luke's telling, Jesus had stepped away from the others to pray when his skin and clothing began to radiate. Meanwhile, the three disciples, like Abraham before the smoking fire pot, had fallen asleep. Ghostly apparitions of Moses and Elijah (representing the law and the prophets, respectively) appear to Jesus and speak with him "about his exodus, which he was about to fulfill in Jerusalem" (Luke 9:31).

While Peter, James, and John behold this glorious manifestation, the mountain peak—like Sinai before it (see chapter 4)—is enshrouded by a great dark cloud. From the depths of this cloud erupts a booming voice, echoing words first spoken at Jesus' baptism in the Jordan River some years earlier: "This is my Son, the Beloved; listen to him!" (Mark 9:7). Schooled in the Scriptures, these disciples could not miss the layered significance of these words. Jesus is the son of YHWH—a title of deep political significance. The son of YHWH represents the inheritor of the Davidic promise; "I will tell of the decree of the LORD: He said to me, 'You are my son; today I have begotten you'" (Ps 2:7).[3] This itinerant preacher has been anointed king. But the resonance of this moment is not restricted to the mundane world of inter-human squabbling; its gravity is cosmic. Standing on a peak, this son of god represents the inversion and overcoming of those other "sons of god" who forged their diabolic plot on Mount Hermon (see chapter 2). Where they represent the powers of violence, greed, and corruption, this son of god incarnates a logic of love, generosity, and justice. Here, on the peak of Mount Tabor, YHWH declares war on the destructive spirit of Babylon in its terrestrial and cosmic guises.

At each of the many mountaintop experiences recounted throughout this book, the protagonist encountered a luminous event. In each case, the thing that glowed was a manifestation of YHWH's presence, what theologians refer to as "theophanic illumination"—the fire pot, the burning bush, the fiery cloud. Here, on Mount Tabor, it is the very flesh of this Galilean preacher that is incandescent with YHWH's presence. Jesus is not a spectator of the glory—he is not Eve and Adam standing before the tree of life, Moses before the burning bush, or the elders at Mount Sinai. He *is* the tree of life. He *is* the burning bush. He *is* the fiery presence.

Six hundred years prior to this encounter, the prophet Ezekiel had a vision of YHWH's glory departing the temple before Nebuchadnezzar's armies ransacked it. Every day since, the Jewish people had anticipated YHWH's return. In this moment, when these three fishermen awake to

---

3. On this point, see Boyarin, *Jewish Gospels*, 26–31.

the spectacle occurring on the mountain, they catch a glimpse of YHWH's glory standing directly before them.

Peter understands what he is experiencing. He sees YHWH. His response is logical: "Rabbi, it is good for us to be here; let us set up three tents" (Matt 17:4). Like David before him, Peter wants to build a temple to house and control the glory. But Jesus refuses. He turns around and leads them back down the mountain. For Jesus, YHWH's glory cannot be contained. Like the tabernacle in the desert, Jesus wants to dwell among the people. On the hike back, he warns the disciples not to speak of what they saw.

8

Golgotha
The Mountain of Death

THE OLD CITY OF Jerusalem is a beautiful tangled maze of narrow alleys, packed to the brim with street vendors. If you can navigate through the shawarma stands, tables of scarves, and barrels of pickled vegetables, you can find the Church of the Holy Sepulchre. Since the fourth century, this has been the traditional pilgrimage location for the crucifixion of Jesus of Nazareth. This, it is said, is Golgotha.

Golgotha (or in Latin, Calvary [*Calvāria*]), the "place of the skull," was a Roman execution site in or near Jerusalem. In the Gospels, this location is described simply as a "place." But for the last fifteen hundred years, this site has traditionally been identified as a hill or a mountain: christened Mount Golgotha (or Mount Calvary). The precise location of Golgotha is disputed. But, in 325 CE, the Christian Roman Empress Helena selected the site upon which the Church of the Holy Sepulchre now sits as the genuine location of Golgotha.

A few hours before Passover, on Golgotha, the blood-caked body of an enigmatic preacher from rural Galilee hangs from a Roman execution cross. A small number of his followers huddle around, sobbing. He held rank in no army. He administered no temple. He wore no crown—spare the bloody twist of thorns now pressed into his head. Nevertheless, above him hangs a small plaque that reads "This is Jesus, the King of the Jews." Jesus of Nazareth is nailed to a tree, lynched in the name of law and order.

POLITICAL STREET THEATER

Passover celebrates the Hebrews' liberation from oppression under the Egyptian pharaoh. It's a religious holiday; but it is also a political holiday, a time to remember the justice of YHWH and the manumission of slaves. It is no wonder that to the Romans, the current occupying empire in Judea, the celebration of Passover is annoying at best and at worst a credible threat. It risks fomenting revolt. The concern is not unfounded. The oppressed citizens of colonized Judea cannot help seeing Rome, like Egypt before it, as an embodiment of the destructive spirit of Babylon. So Passover is a tense time—particularly in Jerusalem, a city rich with religious and political significance since the time of David. Thus, in anticipation of the political fervor, the local governor and his legions parade triumphantly into the city on the first day of the festival, flaunting Roman military might in an effort to discourage insurrection. The message comes through loud and clear: We have the power to wipe you off the map. Don't even think about trying anything.

It's no accident that Jesus selects this same day, the first day of preparation for the Passover, to stage his own anti-triumphal march into the city. Jesus assembles his followers at Bethany, on the opposite side of Jerusalem, and enters the city to cheering crowds proclaiming, "Blessed is the coming kingdom of our ancestor David!" (Mark 11:10). Jesus' parade is satire. To borrow a phrase, it is "political street theater" carefully choreographed to parody the Roman march.[1] The Roman governor processes into the city mounted on a warhorse. Jesus, intentionally evoking imagery from the prophet Zechariah, enters on a colt—a humble farm animal. He exchanges the tools of war for the tools of peace—as Isaiah proclaimed, "they shall beat their swords into plowshares, and their spears into pruning hooks" (Isa 2:4). The Roman governor marches with disciplined, well-armed legions. Jesus parades with a flamboyant band of outcasts and sinners, the poor and the socially marginalized. On opposite sides of Jerusalem, these two parades simultaneously proclaim two counter-kingdoms: one seeks to maintain social cohesion through coercive power, the other—the reign Jesus proclaims—that promises radical social reformation through co-creative participation.

---

1. Here we are following the work of Marcus J. Borg and John Dominic Crossan in *The Last Week*.

RIOTS AND FIGS

Once in the city, Jesus' confrontation with the religious and political powers intensifies. His direct and immediate target is the temple of YHWH. Entering the outer courtyard, Jesus and his followers ransack the temple—flipping the tables of the moneychangers and blocking corridors. Trespassing and vandalism—has the protest march escalated into a full-blown riot? On this busiest and holiest of weeks, Jesus attempts to grind the work of the temple to a halt. He destroys property in the name of justice and shouts at frightened and infuriated onlookers: "Is it not written, 'My house shall be called a house of prayer for all the nations'? But you have made it a den of robbers" (Mark 11:17).

This ostentatious act of aggression is likely what got Jesus killed. But why did he do it? Why attack the holiest site of your own religion on the holiest week of the year? Why draw the watchful eye of Roman soldiers already on high alert and eager to squash anything that smacks of revolt?

Mark gives a clue to Jesus' motivation by bookending this protest with two strange encounters with a fruit tree. Just before entering the temple, Jesus attempts to pick a fig from a nearby tree. Finding no fruit on it, he lashes out at the poor ficus: "May no one ever eat fruit from you again!" (Mark 11:14). Then, after the incident in the temple, the disciples find the tree withered and dead.

Why does Jesus curse a tree? Is he so hungry he can't handle the disappointment of a snack-less fruit tree? Probably not. His unexpected outburst seems all the more bizarre given that Mark tells us explicitly that "it was not the season for figs" (Mark 11:13). The inclusion of this detail suggests that we should avoid reading the story too literally. Jesus is not actually mad at a tree. In the poetic language of the Hebrew Scriptures, the fruit tree is a symbol of the people of YHWH (e.g., Isa 5:1–7; Jer 12:10; Ezek 17:2–10; 19:10–14). When YHWH's people act with justice, the tree is said to bear good fruit. When they oppress or neglect the poor, orphans, widows, and immigrants, it is said that the tree is barren or that its fruit is rotten. So when Mark tells a story about Jesus lashing out at a fig tree and uses that story to frame Jesus' temple riot, he means the tree to be a metaphor for the temple and the religious authorities of Judea. The temple on Mount Zion is supposed to be a new Eden, a tree of life mediating the life-giving energy of YHWH into the world. But this tree is barren. Its fruit is rotten. It is producing injustice.

Another key to understanding Jesus' actions in the temple is his pronouncement: "Is it not written, 'My house shall be called a house of prayer for all the nations'? But you have made it a den of robbers" (Mark 11:17). These words, together with his attack on the moneychangers, are often taken to mean that Jesus disapproved of the buying and selling of commercial goods in the temple. When I (Joe) was a teenager, my youth group had to hold our bake sale in the church parking lot because people in my congregation interpreted Jesus' words in this way and assumed they applied in a straightforward way to our church building as well (though not to the parking lot, apparently). No doubt a healthy skepticism to the insinuation of capitalism into our religious institutions is advisable. And as a rural Galilean who preached against wealth and greed, it is conceivable that the sheer opulence of the temple made Jesus' blood boil. But that's not the point of his protest.

Passover is one of three pilgrimage festivals for which Jews—who by Jesus' day were scattered across the Mediterranean—were encouraged to travel to the temple in Jerusalem to make sacrifices and participate in the festivities. To travel such great distances by foot or by mule while transporting a goat or lamb to be sacrificed in the temple would have proved prohibitively inconvenient for many. Not to mention that on such a journey an animal could easily sustain an injury that would disqualify it from eligibility for sacrifice. So animal vendors in the temple court provided a service essential to the standard operation of the temple and to the celebration of the festival in particular. And because any goods or services exchanged in the temple had to be paid for with a special temple coin—which, in accordance with the law of Moses, bore no graven images—the currency exchange service was a necessary corollary to the animal vendors. The intent of Jesus' protest was to shut down the standard business operations of the temple as prescribed in the law.

If Jesus and his disciples effectively prevented the priests and Levites from carrying sacrificial tools into the inner court (Mark 11:16), then, in addition to shutting down the business office, they may have halted the sacrifices as well. Jesus did not "cleanse the temple" of untoward consumerism, as the headings in many translations of the Bible would mislead us to believe. Like the fig tree, *he symbolically destroyed it*.

Pay attention to the specific language of his pronouncement. He called the temple a *den* of robbers. What does a robber do in his den? A den is not where a robber goes to do his robbing. No, the robber's den is his sanctuary—the safe shelter he retreats to after having robbed someone. Jesus seems to be claiming that the temple is corrupt, not because an injustice is occurring in the temple, but because the temple authorities and Jerusalem aristocracy are exploiting widows, orphans, immigrants, and the poor six days a week and then retreat into the temple on the sabbath to seek the shelter of easy forgiveness or even religious legitimation for their violence.

Interestingly, Jesus wasn't the first to use these words in criticism of the Jerusalem temple. He borrows the phrase from the prophet Jeremiah, who, some six hundred years earlier, gave an impassioned speech at the gates of the first temple, in which he made exactly this point:

> Will you steal, murder, commit adultery, swear falsely, make offerings to Baal, and go after other gods that you have not known and then come and stand before me in this house, which is called by my name, and say, "We are safe!"—only to go on doing all these abominations? Has this house, which is called by my name, become a den of robbers in your sight? (Jer 7:9–11)

According to Jeremiah, the temple of his day had become a place to justify violence and idolatry rather than a place to inspire justice. Shortly thereafter, that temple was demolished by Nebuchadnezzar's armies. Now, six hundred years later, Jesus stands in the outer court of a new temple in the same location, invoking the words of Jeremiah as he signals the destruction of the new temple.

Just as when he offered forgiveness to the paralyzed man, apart from the temple's sacrificial system (see our discussion in chapter 7), he is here again claiming for himself the authority to pass judgment on the temple authorities, who understand *themselves* to be the highest judges.

From the perspective of these religious leaders, this is at best an audacious intrusion and at worst utter blasphemy. Normally, in the eyes of the Romans, a preacher and healer like Jesus would be nothing more than a pest if he blipped onto their radar at all. But his uncanny ability to draw a crowd and his disruptive demonstrations, especially on this volatile week, raises his threat-level to that of a seditious popular leader.

By the combination of his parodic march and his destructive riot, Jesus has symbolically attacked both the political and religious authorities of Jerusalem—two social structures that collude to maintain the oppressive status quo. And so they decide, at least for the moment, to set aside the persistent tensions between them to deal with the troublesome prophet from Galilee. Their determination is swift and brutal—Jesus of Nazareth has to die.

THE MOUNT OF OLIVES

In all four canonical Gospels, Jesus is arrested in a garden called Gethsemane, atop Mount Olivet—a small mountain on the outskirts of Jerusalem. A member of his inner circle—the infamous Judas Iscariot—is bribed by the authorities to betray his whereabouts. They cleverly ambush him when he is isolated from the crowds, who may riot if they see him arrested in public. As the temple police advance toward the mountain, Jesus prays in the garden, begging YHWH that he not have to face this ultimate test.

In the Gospels, Jesus is presented as possessing acute knowledge of his eventual fate. Unsurprisingly, contemporary historians are dubious of such divine premonition (see, e.g., John 12:20–36). But even a secular interpretation of these events could hold that Jesus would plausibly foresee arrest as the likely outcome of his protest march in Bethany and his riot in the temple. Marguerite Porete and Thomas Muntzer, Nat Turner and John Brown, Oscar Romero and Harvey Milk—prophets of every age have paid the price of their liberative action in blood. Each in their own way could echo the words of Martin Luther King Jr.: "I've seen the Promised Land. I may not get there with you."[2] Whatever else Jesus may have known, he certainly was aware of the fate of the prophets. To him, Jerusalem was "the city that kills the prophets and stones those who are sent to it!" (Matt 23:37). And he entered this powder keg knowing what was at stake.

As Jesus mournfully prays, an armed posse ascends the mountain, led by his own disciple and friend. With a kiss, Judas identifies Jesus. He is arrested and hauled off for trial before the Jewish court of the Sanhedrin. Having been betrayed by one, his other male disciples abandon him and flee into the night. Alone, Jesus is escorted away to his sham trial.

ARE YOU THE MESSIAH?

At his religious trial before the Sanhedrin, Jesus is pressed with a seemingly simple interrogation: "Are you the messiah?" (Mark 14:61) This, it turns out, is a loaded question. As discussed in the previous chapter, the figure

---

2. King, "I've Been to the Mountaintop."

of a messiah—one who would play the dual role of religious prophet and political liberator—was a common image of the Second Temple period. The messiah, it was suggested, would both guide the Jewish people back to the correct form of religious observance and, as a type of Davidic king, would redeem the people from bondage to foreign rulers—in this context, the Roman Empire. The question is designed to doubly entrap Jesus. Theologically, the self-declaration would mark Jesus as a dangerous usurper of YHWH's divine authority to name the messiah. Politically, it would mark him as an insurrectionist, a challenge to Roman imperial authority in the colonized Judea. Despite these dual risks, Jesus responds to the question simply and directly: "I am" (Mark 14:62). This two-word response not only answers the direct question, but also invokes YHWH's response to Moses at the burning bush (see chapter 4). The Sanhedrin does not miss this subtlety. Recognizing Jesus' claim to divine authority, they immediately declare him a blasphemer, beat him, and condemn him to death.

Unfortunately for this religious court, local religious leaders do not have the authority to impose the death sentence. And so, the Sanhedrin use their local clout with an already nervous empire to convince Pilate, the Roman governor of Judea, to take on Jesus' case as an imperial trial.

Like the Sanhedrin, Pilate opens this Roman trial with a direct but loaded question: "Are you the king of the Jews?" The political significance is palpable. Pilate does not care about blasphemy, he wants to know if Jesus will upset the precarious Jerusalem situation by challenging Roman authority. Roman propaganda promised two things: peace and security. A popular uprising threatens both. Unlike at his trial before the Sanhedrin, Jesus responds to Pilate's opaquely: "You say so" (Mark 15:2).

This response is savvy. Pilate is seeking to condemn Jesus for sedition. But Jesus is playing a different political game. Jesus is a king and Jesus is not a king. He refuses to say "yes" because, in Pilate's mind, that would be an admission of insurrectionary aspirations. Jesus has no intention of building an army and overthrowing Roman rule. But he also refuses to say "no" because, in a deeper sense, he truly does aim to restructure political life. Jesus' mission is the inauguration of the reign of YHWH—a mission which, despite two millennia of attempts to domesticate it through over-spiritualization, is both spiritual *and political*. The reign of YHWH is spiritual because it signifies the return of YHWH from exile. It is thus, not merely one more kingdom that stands among the others—the next in an unbroken chain of empires. But it is also political because the return of

Golgotha

YHWH to Zion implies the genuine overthrow of every manifestation of the spirit of Babylon, the imperial powers of every age.

At least according to Mark, the oldest surviving account of the trial, this enigmatic reply is the only response Jesus offers in the interrogation. From this point forward, he chooses to remain silent. This silence stuns the governor and places him in a bind. He can't afford to look weak on insurrection. But he also seems not to consider Jesus a credible political threat. So, looking for a loophole, Pilate plays the beneficent ruler and makes the community an offer. In recognition of Passover, he is willing to release Jesus. "Do you want me to release for you the king of the Jews?" (Mark 15:9), he asks. But the religious authorities have stirred up the assembled crowd in favor of another prisoner on death row, an anti-Roman revolutionary named Barabbas. Outsmarted, Pilate reluctantly submits to the will of the crowd.[3] What then should be done with this so-called "king of the Jews?" Pilate asks. The crowd responds in a single voice: "Crucify him!"

THE PLACE OF THE SKULL

Roman soldiers strip, flog, and mock Jesus. Highlighting the political edge of this execution, they garb him in a purple cloak (a royal color) and twist a crown of thorns into his head. They sarcastically declare "Hail, the king of the Jews!" between strikes and blows. Once they tire of this sadistic torture, they strip off his "royal garments" and lead him off to be crucified.

They take Jesus up to Golgotha, the place of the skull, the Roman execution site. There, between two anti-Roman insurrectionists, they unceremoniously nail him to a cross. Then, in a manner that the early Christians could not but see as a terrible inversion of an enthronement ceremony for a new king, they raise him up, not onto a throne, but onto an executioner's

---

3. The Gospel texts go to great lengths to distance Pilate from culpability in the execution of Jesus. They did so for reasons that are completely understandable in the first-century context in which they were written. The early Christians lived under Roman occupation; it would be dangerous to frame their occupiers as committing this great crime. Unfortunately, the literary decision to shift responsibility from Rome to the temple leaders had a result that was completely unforeseeable to the largely Jewish early Christian community: it provided fodder to the later anti-Semitic slander of Jews as "Christ killers." As a result, responsible biblical scholars have both a historical and a moral duty to be clear—*the Romans* killed Jesus. He was executed by the imperial state for the crime of insurrection. On this, see Crossan, *Who Killed Jesus?*

rack. The plaque publicizing his charges reads: "the king of the Jews" (Mark 15:26).

Three loyal women—Mary Magdalene, Mary the mother of James and Joses, and Salome—the few disciples who remain by his side, can only watch as Jesus bleeds out on the cross. "How," they must be asking themselves, "can Jesus inaugurate the reign of YHWH, if he has been mocked, beaten, and crucified?" How can a dying, tortured man be the return of YHWH's glory if, as Deuteronomy says, "anyone hung on a tree is under God's curse" (Deut 21:23)? Jesus himself cries out: "My God, My God, Why have you forsaken me?" (Mark 15:34) This is the paradox at the heart of the Gospel of Mark. As Jesus lets out a loud cry and breathes his last breath, hanging like a lynched body from a tree, the reader is faced with the question Jesus put to his disciples: "Who do you say that I am?" (Mark 8:29)

Mark signifies this explosive reality through a cosmic upheaval: the tearing of the curtain enclosing the holy of holies in the temple. The veil separating the heavens and the earth has been torn in two. "Thy kingdom come, thy will be done, on earth as it is in heaven" (Matt 6:10). But the disturbing reality of this cosmic upheaval is that there is nothing there. No fiery presence. No great cloud. Nothing. The holy of holies is empty. As the priests, Levites, and heads of families in Ezra 3 already knew, the glory has not returned to the temple. It is absent. It remains in exile. The glory has not been contained. It is not carefully stage-managed by the religious authorities, who appear rather like the Great and Powerful Oz, desperately pleading, "Pay no attention to that man behind the curtain."[4]

The glory of YHWH is not locked up safe in a temple because, at that precise moment, it is dying on the cross. YHWH's glory is caked in blood and nailed to a tree. The glory is dying in solidarity with the poor and the oppressed masses, colonized and victimized by the combined forces of religious and political authority. This is the ultimate inversion of the upside-down reign of YHWH. Divine power and wonder have been set aside for a harder path. In the words of Paul:

> Though he existed in the form of God,
>   he did not regard equality with God
>   as something to be grasped,
> but emptied himself,
>   taking the form of a slave,
>   assuming human likeness.

4. On this theme, see Rollins, *Divine Magician*, ch. 3.

Golgotha

> And being found in appearance as a human,
> > he humbled himself
> > and became obedient to the point of death—
> > even death on a cross. (Phil 2:6–8)

This is the radicality of the gospel: divine glory appears without light or power, clothed in neither royal garb nor priestly vestments, but in the all-too-human reality of suffering and death at the hands of an unjust colonizing empire. In this ultimate act of incarnation, transcendence is emptied into the immanence and flesh of the world. In the words of Friedrich Nietzsche, "Gods too decompose. God is dead. God remains dead. And we have killed him."[5] This, the theologian Thomas Altizer suggests, is the terrifying atheism at the heart of Christianity. "We must recognize," he writes, "that the proclamation of the death of God is a Christian confession of faith, and of a uniquely Christian faith in the ultimacy of the Crucifixion."[6]

In Mark's characteristic irony, it is not a priest or a Levite, a disciple or a prophet who experiences the cosmic weight of this execution. It is a Roman occupier, an enemy of YHWH's people if ever there was one. It is one of Jesus' executioners who first recognizes the terrifying confluence: the bloody corpse of this executed convict *is* the glory of YHWH. He exclaims, "Truly this man is the son of God" (Mark 15:39).

---

5. Nietzsche, *Gay Science*, 181.

6. Altizer, *New Gospel of Christian Atheism*. It should not be forgotten that Nietzsche, that arch-heretic, retrieved the infamous words "God is dead" (by way of G. W. F. Hegel) from the Lutheran composer Johann von Rist's 1641 hymn, *Ein trauriger Grabgesang*, which mournfully sings: "God himself is dead / He died on the cross."

9

Olivet
The Mountain of Absence

IN EAST JERUSALEM, IN the Palestinian West Bank, you can find a small mountain ridge. Named for the olive groves that once covered it, Mount Olivet has been a historically significant site for thousands of years. Having played an important role in a number of key narratives in Jesus' life, the mountain has become a popular pilgrimage location. Mount Olivet should perhaps be known as a mountain of mourning. It was there that David fled from his rebellious son, Absalom, and cried as he ascended. It was there that Jesus wept for the city of Jerusalem. And it was there that, on the night before his arrest, Jesus cried in the garden of Gethsemane. Today, you could visit a variety of religious sites, including a three-thousand-year-old Jewish cemetery, multiple churches dedicated to the ascension of Jesus, and a Latter Day Saints university.

On this mountaintop, forty days after his execution by the occupying Roman forces, Jesus of Nazareth stands together with his assembled disciples. These disciples have been through a lot. They've left their families and friends to follow an itinerant preacher out of the backwater of Galilee into the heart of Roman Judea. They've seen miraculous things they can't explain. They've heard difficult teachings that have challenged them to live into a radical ethic of care for the poor and the marginalized and exploded their sense of ethnic and religious identity. But for them, this is an interim ethic, the calm before the storm. This has all been preparation for the revelation of Jesus as the messiah, the one who will overthrow the Romans and re-establish the Davidic kingdom. And so they ask, "Lord, is this the time when you will restore the kingdom to Israel?" But Jesus dodges the question: "It is not for you to know the times or periods that the Father has set by his own authority." Instead of an answer, Jesus gives them an itinerary: "You will receive power when the Holy Spirit has come upon you, and you will be my witnesses in Jerusalem, in all Judea and Samaria, and to the ends of the earth" (Acts 1:6–8). With these words, Jesus ascends into the heavens, leaving his disciples staring dumbfounded into the sky.

But wait. How is this conversation happening? How is Jesus ascending anywhere? Didn't he just die—executed by the state? We need to rewind a few weeks.

THE ROAD TO EMMAUS

Jesus is dead. He's been executed on the order of the Roman governor Pontius Pilate. One of his former followers, Cleopas, is processing the events that transpired in Jerusalem and led to Jesus' brutal execution with his companion as the pair walk toward Emmaus and away from their messianic hopes. Somewhere along the way, a stranger sidles up to them and strikes up a conversation. But the grieving disciples are in no mood for small talk. Picking up on their mournfulness, the stranger asks them what's the matter. They tell him about Jesus, how his miracles and teaching suggested that he was a messianic hopeful; how they had believed that he would be the one to finally oust the Roman occupation and restore the kingdom of Israel to her former glory; and how, instead, their own religious leaders had handed him over to the occupying forces to be executed.

For the remainder of the walk, "beginning with Moses and all the prophets, he interpreted to them the things about himself in all the scriptures" (Luke 24:27). He speaks, no doubt, of creation and revolt, both cosmic and human; of the smoking fire pot passing through the covenant sacrifices as Abraham slept under a tree, and of YHWH's rescue of Their people from slavery in Egypt; of kings, temples, and exile; of the fire in the burning bush and atop Mount Sinai. The travelers would later recount that as he was teaching them these things, a fire began to burn in their own hearts—perhaps that same fire. Throughout his exposition, the stranger is keen to demonstrate that their hopes for the renewal of the covenant need not have died with their teacher. Rather, he argues, the Scriptures point to a messiah whose work would be accomplished through suffering, perhaps even through death.

When they arrive in Emmaus the couple invite their new traveling companion to stay with them for the night before he continues on with the rest of his journey. When they sit down to dinner the stranger takes the bread from the table, says a blessing over it, breaks it, and gives it to his hosts. Suddenly, they realize that their guest is Jesus himself. He's alive! How is this possible? And then, in the very moment that they finally recognize him, and just as suddenly, he vanishes from their sight.

ON RESURRECTION

The idea of resurrection developed in Jewish theology sometime after the Babylonian exile. In most of the Tanakh, everyone who dies—righteous and unrighteous alike—goes to a shadowy underworld called *Sheol*. *Sheol* probably first referred to the literal hole in the ground in which a corpse was laid (see Pss 16:10; 49:14). In fact, you could go there before death if you got buried alive (Num 16:31–33). One should not confuse *Sheol* with the medieval Christian notion of hell, a place of punishment or torment. Rather, *Sheol* is a "land of forgetfulness" (Ps 88:12). The dead do not even know that they are there (Eccl 9:5); not even YHWH remembers them (Ps 88:4–5).[1]

In exile, though, the prophet Ezekiel has a dream. In it, he is walking the perimeter of a valley filled with dead, dry bones, when the voice of YHWH tells him to prophesy to the bones. The prophet does as he is told. "Suddenly," he recounts, "there was a noise, a rattling, and the bones came together, bone to its bone . . . [then] sinews on them, and flesh had come upon them, and skin had covered them" (Ezek 37:7–8). Next, the voice of YHWH tells him to prophesy to the four winds. When he does, breath comes into these zombies and they stand, a great army of the living.

---

1. Not every ancient Israelite held the same beliefs about the afterlife (or non-afterlife, as the case may be), any more than every modern American does. The Torah prohibits the use of mediums to summon the dead (Lev 19:31; Deut 18:10). You don't make a law against something that no one is doing. So, obviously, some ancient Israelites believed that some part of a person survived her death and could be summoned. There is one ghost story in the Tanakh, in which, despite the prohibition, King Saul employs a medium to channel the prophet Samuel from the grave. When Samuel comes out of the grave (visible only to the medium) he is annoyed at having been disturbed from his rest (1 Sam 28).

Ezekiel's dream is a metaphor, as dreams are wont to be. It signifies that YHWH will rescue Their people from exile in Babylon and return them to their homeland. YHWH says as much in the dream itself:

> Mortal, these bones are the whole house of Israel. They say, "Our bones are dried up, and our hope is lost; we are cut off completely." . . . [But] I am going to open your graves and bring you up from your graves, O my people, and I will bring you back to the land of Israel. . . . I will put my spirit within you, and you shall live, and I will place you on your own soil. (Ezek 37:11–14)

But by Jesus' day, many Jews had developed Ezekiel's dream image into a full-blown belief that the bodies of righteous followers of YHWH would be resurrected at the end of the age (Dan 12:2). Jesus himself affirms this view against the more theologically conservative Sadducees, who reject any such idea of resurrection (Mark 12:18–27).

Following their rabbi, almost all of the earliest Christians latch onto the narrative of resurrection, but with one important twist. As the New Testament scholar N. T. Wright points out, for early Christians, "the resurrection, as an event, has split into two."[2] The non-Christian Jews of the first century who believed in a resurrection—such as the Pharisees—anticipated it as something that would happen to all of YHWH's people, or perhaps even *all people*, at the inauguration of the reign of YHWH on earth. But what we find in early Christianity, as Wright points out, is "the belief that the mode of this inauguration consisted in the resurrection itself happening to one person in the middle of history in advance of its great, final occurrence."[3] The resurrection of Jesus is, to borrow a metaphor from Paul, the "first fruits" of a harvest that remains yet to come (1 Cor 15:20), the down payment on the great resurrection of all, which will come at the end of history.

FIRST FRUITS

As the first fruits of the resurrection, the Gospel narratives present a variety of stories about the resurrected Jesus. Mark, the earliest of the canonical Gospels, originally ended rather abruptly. The Sunday after Jesus' execution, the women who witnessed his death return to the tomb. Where they

---

2. Wright, *Surprised by Hope*, 44–45.
3. Wright, *Surprised by Hope*, 45.

expect to find the body of their teacher, they instead discover an empty tomb and a mysterious young man dressed in a radiant white. He declares that Jesus cannot be found in the tomb: "He has been raised; he is not here" (Mark 16:8). The response of the women is understandable. They run away: "Terror and amazement had seized them, and they said nothing to anyone" (Mark 16:8). Cut to black, roll credits.

The early church seems to have found this ending a bit too jarring and narratively unsatisfying, so they added two longer endings. First, a brief concluding paragraph pointed toward the spread of the growing community (Mark 16:9–11). Later still, an even longer ending was added (Mark 16:12–20). Here, Jesus appears to the Twelve, commissions them to spread his message of the reign of YHWH to all creation, and then ascends to the heavens.

The later Gospels provide more robust accounts of Jesus' various post-resurrectional adventures. Matthew includes a mountaintop commission. Luke adds the story of the two mourning disciples described above, as well as a short meal intended to prove that he is not a ghost (apparently ghosts don't eat). But it is the Fourth Gospel, the Gospel according to John, that provides the most detailed narrative. There, Jesus has a short dialogue in the garden with Mary, appears to the disciples in an upper room, returns for an encounter with Thomas—who famously doubts his compatriots' story—provides the disciples with a miraculous catch of fish, and appoints Peter as the leader of the new community. This Johannine resurrected Christ is much busier than his Markan counterpart.

YOU WILL NOT ALWAYS HAVE ME

The resurrection story culminates at the mountaintop encounter with which this chapter began. Jesus gives a final charge to his loyal disciples, before floating off into the heavens. Despite minor discrepancies among the Gospels (as well as Acts), this is the basic narrative of what Christians would come to know as "the ascension."

But there is a tension in this story. It's a wonderful image, a bit of magical realism as some guy floats up into the clouds. But wasn't the whole point of the Gospels the incarnation—"Emmanuel; God with us"? In Jesus, YHWH enters into the complicated, messy reality of the world. The incarnation is YHWH saying, "I won't watch from the sidelines, I'll get into the muck myself." But then Jesus just packs his bags and floats away? YHWH was supposed to defeat empire, but now the disciples find themselves sitting alone in the dirt, staring up into the sky with dumb looks on their faces. The reign of YHWH was supposed to answer the problem of exile. But they are left alone—again.

At this point, one of the disciples might have recalled an event from the final week of Jesus' life. A woman anointed him with some very expensive oil, dumping out the whole bottle. Some of Jesus' disciples are understandably upset by this extravagant gesture. They protest that the ointment could have been sold and the proceeds given to the poor. This seems like an admirable bit of social-justice thinking. But Jesus surprisingly tells the disciples to stop bothering the woman, "For you always have the poor with you, but you will not always have me" (Matt 26:11).

This is a strange thing for Jesus to say. Just two chapters later he will seemingly contradict himself, declaring: "I am with you always, to the end of the age" (Matt 28:20). Well, which is it? Is he here or is he gone? Christians have tended to stick to Matthew 28:20. "I am with you always" looks good on a bumper sticker. Nobody wants a bumper sticker that essentially says, "You are all alone." But Jesus says exactly that. Indeed, he promises it. Jesus promises that there is a time when the disciples will have to go it alone.[4]

Even more bafflingly, what does any of this have to do with the poor? Christians have often abused Jesus' words here. "Jesus said the poor will always be around," I (Justin) often heard as a kid, "so why invest in welfare or social programs?" But this entirely misses the radical point that Jesus is making. It's easy to read this passage in the abstract. "The poor will always be with you" sounds like it could mean "there will always be poor people." But Jesus' "with you" is saying something more specific. He isn't simply saying "poor people will exist on the earth"; he's setting a vocation. He's saying the poor will be with *you*, with *this community*. The people of the reign of YHWH are to be those who live with and among the downtrodden and the marginalized. Jesus seems to be saying that although he won't always be here, the disciples will be busy with an important task: building the reign of YHWH among the outcasts.

Reassembling the two halves of Jesus' statement, then, we might describe the reign of YHWH as *a community who lives in the absence of Jesus and in the presence of the poor*. It is this vocation that so often gets overwritten by concerns with "missions" or "spreading the gospel." The church has

---

4. For this insight, we are indebted to Mark Allen Powell. See his *Loving Jesus*, 54–56.

often anxiously directed itself to expansion-at-all-costs, as though the reign of YHWH was a multi-level marketing scheme. But the true vocation is a more difficult one, indeed it is a cosmic vocation. In Judaism, this task has often gone by the name *tikkun olam*, "repairing the world." It is the renewal of all creation. The community's task is not to ascend to the top of the cosmic mountain with Jesus, but rather to descend ever deeper into the flesh of the world.

This is the paradox of Jesus' assertion that "where two or three are gathered in my name, I am there among them" (Matt 18:20). To gather in someone's name is precisely to gather in their absence, *in memoriam*. "Do this in remembrance of me" (Luke 22:19). But it is through this absence—or more precisely, *through the communal gathering in the midst of that absence*—that the spirit of YHWH is made paradoxically present. It is this difficult task that the earliest followers of Jesus sought to undertake, gathered together in an upper room in Jerusalem to celebrate *Shavuot*.

WIND AND FIRE

Shavuot is the Jewish harvest festival, when the first fruits of the grain harvest are paraded into the temple in ornate gold and silver baskets on the backs of oxen to be offered as a sacrifice of thanksgiving. In English, *Shavuot* is often called "the Feast of Weeks," as it comes forty-nine days—a week of weeks—after Passover. In modern times, these forty-nine days have become a time of mourning for the lives lost during the *Shoah* and other acts of anti-Semitic violence.

Since *Shavuot* is one of three pilgrimage festivals, during which observant Jews are encouraged to travel to Jerusalem, the disciples all got together to celebrate. So there they are eating breakfast, probably after having stayed up late into the night drinking and rehashing old stories, when "suddenly . . . there came a sound like the rush of a violent wind, and it filled the entire house" (Acts 2:2).

Wind evokes countless stories of YHWH's encounters with the world. There is the *wind* that swept over the waters of creation (Gen 1:2); the *breath* to which Ezekiel prophesied and which came from the four winds to bring new life into dry bones (Ezek 37:9–10); the *breath* with which YHWH breathed life into Adam's nostrils (Gen 2:7) and with which Jesus imparted the spirit of YHWH to his disciples (John 20:22).

But the disciples have scant time to reflect on the symbolic resonances of this miraculous wind. For immediately, an eerie phantasm appears in the room. The King James Version adroitly translates this manifestation as "cloven tongues like as of fire" which "sat upon each of them" (Acts 2:3).

Weirdly, the text doesn't indicate that anyone freaks out about the fire. Their hair and clothes are not singed. It's a strange kind of fire. Just like the fire that Moses noticed in the bush on Mount Sinai, this fire burns without consuming what it's burning. It is the same fire that, as a smoking fire pot, passed between the covenant sacrifices while Abraham was fast asleep. It is the pillar of fire that the people of Israel followed around the wilderness and made its home in the tabernacle. It is the incandescent light that shone through Jesus' skin and clothes on Mount Tabor.

But this fire is also different. This fire isn't one; it is many. These multitudinous fires come and rest upon each of the disciples. In the Pentecost experience, the disciples encounter a divine presence that is not restricted to a burning bush. It is not contained by the tabernacle or the temple. It is not locked in a holy of holies. It is not trapped at the inaccessible peak of a mountaintop. Indeed, it is not even contained in the person of Jesus. On this day, Jesus' disciples experience the radical horizontality of a spirit that is suffused throughout creation. They experience a spirit that refuses to be just one thing to just one people. They experience the material embodiment of the radical words of Jesus—"the kingdom of God is among you" (Luke 17:21).

This wind and flame attract attention and a crowd begins to gather around the house. Remember, *Shavuot* is a pilgrimage festival. So there are Jews and converts from every ethnic group throughout Mesopotamia and around the Mediterranean all staying in Jerusalem. Everyone who had gathered around the house is shocked because they hear the people inside speaking but they each hear the conversation in their own native language.

This doesn't appear to be glossolalia—a widely attested trans-religious phenomenon in which one fluidly vocalizes syllable-like sounds with no readily comprehensible meaning, known colloquially as "speaking in tongues."[5] The Pentecost experience is exactly the opposite: *everyone*—re-

---

5. It seems that some people practiced glossolalia in the churches started by Paul. We know that Paul himself did (1 Cor 14:18). And it seems to be what he was referring to when he talked about speaking "in the tongues of humans and angels" (1 Cor 13:1), or when he says that when one does not know what to pray "the Spirit intercedes with groanings too deep for words" (Rom 8:26). But for Paul, glossolalia was to be used primarily as a private prayer language (1 Cor 14:2). If it was ever spoken in public, it needed to be interpreted for people to understand what was being said (1 Cor 12:10).

gardless of where they came from or what language they speak—can understand what is being said.

Here we see a narrative reversal of the tower of Babel. The construction of a counterfeit cosmic mountain at Babylon symbolized an all-too-human hubris—the desire to seize coercive power, to build our way into the heavens (see chapter 2). But coercive power fragments the world into distrust and division, symbolized by the confusion of languages. We see this spirit of Babylon at work everywhere that power-grabbing politicians and religious leaders use their words to twist and distort reality. When wars of aggression are called "peacekeeping missions," when Christian nationalism is disguised as "religious liberty," when policies of hate and bigotry are passed off as "family values." These are the babbling words of Babylon. In such a state we are no longer able to hear and understand one another. Community is ruptured into "us" and "them." But at Pentecost, the spirit of YHWH condescends from the heavens to overcome the divisions of language, to provoke co-creativity and mutual understanding. Pentecost seeks to mend what Babel tore asunder.

This kind of unity is as challenging as it is attractive. Splitting the world into neat categories of friends and enemies, us and them, is easy. It is tidy. Building bridges *across* difference—without repeating colonialist gestures that only *erase* difference—is hard. Creating a genuinely multi-ethnic community is hard. This was no less true for these early Christians than it is today.

A DREAM AND A DEBATE

The Pentecost experience leads the earliest Jesus followers—all ethnically Jewish—not only to cross the aisle *within* their own religious tradition, but to entirely reconceive ethnic and religious boundaries.

One day, a short time after this Pentecost experience, Peter is sitting on the roof of his friend Simon's beach-side home in Jaffa. While he is watching the waves and praying, Peter falls into a meditative trance. He begins to see visions: the skies open and a huge sheet descends from the heavens. On it are hosts of unkosher animals—reptiles and carrion-eating birds. He is aghast to hear a voice say, "Get up, Peter; kill and eat." "I have never eaten anything that is profane or unclean," he shouts back. But the voice is insistent. It replies, "What God has made clean, you must not call profane" (Acts 10:13–15). We're told that the conversation takes place *three times* in the dream before he wakes up.[6] Peter understands the seriousness of what is being asked; it is not a command he can take lightly.

Peter is reflecting on what this dream could possibly have meant when he hears a knock at the door. Imagine his surprise—and perhaps terror—when his host tells him that it is Roman soldiers. Have they come to execute him as they did his rabbi? But strangely, the soldiers instead report that they are here to invite Peter to a dinner party with an Italian centurion named Cornelius. Cornelius, even though he's Roman, is an admirer of Judaism and wants to hear about Peter's faith.

This is a big ask for Peter. In the Hellenistic period, it was uncommon for Jews to eat with gentiles or to eat food prepared by gentiles. Not only has Peter never eaten unkosher animals like those that descended on the sheet in his vision; it is likely he has never had a meal with a gentile, let alone an agent of the occupying empire.

In this moment, Peter realizes what his dream was about. He is not being called to eat pork or lobster; he's being called to go with these men, to have dinner with Cornelius, and to tell him about the reign of YHWH and the renewal of all things. So Peter does just that. Not only does he eat with these gentiles, but, recognizing the spirit of YHWH within them, he baptizes Cornelius and his party guests.

When Peter recognizes the gentile Cornelius and inducts him into the community through the initiation ritual of baptism, he radically redefines the boundaries of inclusion. This move is not without controversy. Some other followers of Jesus are teaching a more traditional message: that "unless you are circumcised according to the custom of Moses, you cannot be saved" (Acts 15:1). Today, even though there are in fact some one-and-a-half-million Jewish Christians, some people wonder whether it is possible to become a Christian and remain Jewish. But in the middle of the first century the question was exactly the opposite: Can someone be a follower of the way of Jesus if they are not Jewish? This ensuing debate would take decades of the movement's formative years and occupy much of the New Testament.

The debate comes to a head at a gathering of the movement's most important leaders, known to history as the Council of Jerusalem. According to the account of the council in the book of Acts, the decisive moment in the debate is Peter's testimony. Peter reports that Cornelius and other

---

6. Threefold repetition is something of a pattern for Peter when he doesn't get what's going on. See Mark 14:66–72; John 21:15–19.

gentiles have committed themselves to Christ and received the same gift of the spirit of YHWH the Jewish followers had on the day of Pentecost. According to Peter, this is sufficient evidence that YHWH "has made no distinction between them and us" (Acts 15:9). Paul and Barnabas, a couple of missionaries who had likewise been announcing the news about Jesus among the gentiles, share similar stories. Finally, James, Jesus' brother and the de facto leader of the movement, makes the final call, demanding that people "not trouble those gentiles who are turning to God" (Acts 15:19).[7]

PAUL'S COMPLEX COMMUNITIES

Of course, this sort of radical subversion of social and ethnic boundaries comes with its difficulties. To hear the early convert and missionary Paul tell the story, shortly after the agreement, James reneges on his decision at the council. He sends missionaries to the churches that Paul started around the Mediterranean to tell the gentile congregants that, if they want to be followers of the reign of YHWH, they must first convert to Judaism, being marked by the ritual of circumcision. Even Peter—the champion of gentile inclusion at the council—stops sharing meals with gentile Christians in an

---

7. A similar debate rages in churches today, though it is not concerned with circumcision and the kosher foods, but with sexuality and gender identity. Should queer folks be granted full participation in the life and ministries of the church? There is no question that Paul and other early church leaders condemned certain forms of sexuality and gender expression that were coded as aberrant in their day. Some argue that these condemnations ought to apply directly to queer folks today. They use these "clobber passages" to bar queer Christians from receiving the sacrament of marriage and from serving in leadership roles in the church. This position has even influenced modern translations of the Bible to the extent that modern words like "homosexuality" are used to (mis)translate Paul's ancient-world concepts, which are entirely foreign to us. On this, see the documentary *1946: The Mistranslation That Shifted Culture*, directed by Sharon Roggio.

One thing is clear: there are queer folks who have committed themselves to Christ and who demonstrate signs of the gifting of the spirit of YHWH. If we are to follow Peter's argument and the decision of the Council of Jerusalem as it pertained to gentiles, then this is evidence that this spirit has made no distinction. If enthusiastic conversion and the work of the spirit was enough for Peter, Paul, and James, then it makes little sense for cisgender and heterosexual Christians to debate whether to "welcome" queer folks into the church. For there has never been any version of the church in which queer folks were not already included—they've always been here, sitting in the pews, preaching from the pulpits, serving at the altars. There is no "us" apart from a "them" to do the welcoming. "They" are "us." This is the radical message of the council of Jerusalem.

attempt to appease the more traditionally minded of his Jewish-Christian compatriots.

If James and Peter really did have such a dramatic change of heart, we'll never know why; no extant document records their side of the story. It's possible that Luke (the name traditionally given to the author of Acts) overstated the initial consensus at the Council of Jerusalem. Or maybe Paul overstated the offense of his theological opponents. Whatever the details, Paul and Peter have it out at Antioch.

Paul argues that "a person is justified not by the works of the law but through the faith of Jesus Christ" (Gal 2:16). That is to say, one is marked as a member of YHWH's partnership by trust and commitment, not by ritual markers like circumcision. In defense of this position, he invokes the paradigmatic figure of Jewish faithfulness: Abraham. When Abraham first received the covenant, Paul notes, he was not yet circumcised. He *first* had to trust YHWH's promises and commit himself to the mission of blessing the nations *before* he ritually entered into the law. Indeed, the law itself would not be fully codified for another four centuries. And yet, this act of trust was counted as an act of justice (Gal 3:6; cf. Gen 15:6). Therefore, in the same way, Paul says, gentiles who commit themselves to the reign of YHWH can be fully adopted as members of the covenant (Gal 4:5), the way a foreign branch can be grafted into an existing tree (Rom 11:17).

It is this radically inclusive position that led the philosopher Alain Badiou to name Paul the "foundation of universalism."[8] And this universalist position ultimately won the day. Perhaps it won because of Paul's convincing theological arguments; perhaps because Paul was a more effective missionary; or perhaps because less than two generations after the founding of the Jerusalem church, an uprising would break out in Judea and the Roman war machine would respond with overwhelming force, eviscerating the city of Jerusalem and killing much of the Jewish-Christian leadership. Whatever the reason, by the close of the first century, the majority of Christians would be gentiles—and the church would be an irreversibly multi-ethnic community. At the heart of this theology is a reconception of the covenant partnership by which Abraham was called. This covenant is larger than Abraham or his descendants alone, larger than any ethnic or religious identity. The purpose of the covenant is the blessing of all the nations (Gen 12:3), the reconciliation of all things. It is the culmination of the difficult vocation Jesus gave his disciples on the top of Mount Olivet:

---

8. Badiou, *Saint Paul: The Foundation of Universalism*.

"you will receive power when the Holy Spirit has come upon you, and you will be my witnesses in Jerusalem, in all Judea and Samaria, and *to the ends of the earth*" (Acts 1:8).

10

The New Eden
The Mountain of Re-Creation

EDEN IS NOT A geological formation. You can't scale the face of Mount Eden. It isn't renowned for tourism or skiing. It's not home to a culinary delicacy or the site of a famous ancient battle. Unlike other cosmic mountains in the biblical texts—like Hermon, Tabor, or Zion—you can't make a pilgrimage to Eden. While the exact locations of Moriah, Sinai, or Golgotha are disputed, few would deny that the texts are invoking real places. Eden is different. If the authors of the biblical text had a real Mount Eden in mind, that referent has long since been lost. But the authorial choice to describe the mountain as the head of four rivers, which are, in reality, hundreds or thousands of miles apart, strongly suggests that it was never intended to be taken literally. Eden is a myth. It is a theological symbol, a truly cosmic mountain. It is not only the home of the mythic past, it also points forward to a mythic future. Eden is the symbol of the cosmos set right.

In the beginning, the heavens and the earth were united at the garden temple on the mountain of Eden. There, the life-giving divine energy flowed freely from the tree of life. But this Edenic peace was shattered by a tragic misstep. Subsequently, the desire to seize power resulted in a cosmic disaster—indeed, a series of cosmic disasters: a revolt in the heavens, violence and death upon the earth, empires, exiles, and occupations. The potentiality of Eden, everything that the world could have been, was thrown into disarray.

In response, YHWH partnered with one family, the family of Abraham and Sarah. This family would become the instrument of reconciliation for all nations. It is through them, YHWH promises, that "all the families of the earth shall be blessed" (Gen 12:3). This covenantal promise was sealed on Mount Moriah and renewed on Mount Sinai. There, the people of YHWH were called to be set apart as a priestly kingdom. Just as a priest guides their flock, the people of YHWH are tasked with guiding the nations in reconciliation with the creator.

But Abraham's family wanted to "be like other nations" (1 Sam 8:20); it quickly succumbed to the corrupting spirit of Babylon—that quiet voice within every soul and every nation that craves power and control at any cost. Thus, rather than a holy nation and a priestly kingdom guiding all peoples toward reconciliation, under their monarchs, the people of YHWH descended into precisely the slavery, greed, and civil war that they were supposed to overcome. This path of violence eventuated in exile and despair.

And so, in the midst of this exilic condition, the genuine prophets of YHWH imagined a day of true reconciliation, *not only for the people of YHWH*, but—evoking that ancient promise to Sarah and Abraham—also for the reconciliation of all nations. As the prophet Micah prophesied:

> In days to come
>   the mountain of the LORD's temple
> shall be established as the highest of the mountains
>   and shall be raised up above the hills.
> Peoples shall stream to it,
>   and many nations shall come and say:
> "Come, let us go up to the mountain of the LORD,
>   to the house of the God of Jacob,
> that he may teach us his ways
>   and that we may walk in his paths." (Mic 4:1–2)

This is the apocalyptic "Day of YHWH." This vision soon expanded to a cosmic scale, such that these prophets could not only imagine the reconciliation of all nations, *but of all things*. On this great Day, YHWH would intervene into history to set all things right. Peace and prosperity would reign until even "the wolf shall live with the lamb; the leopard shall lie down with the kid; the calf and the lion will feed together, and a little child shall lead them" (Isa 11:6). On this great Day, the nations would stream back to the life-giving holy mountain of YHWH. As the prophet Isaiah writes:

> In days to come the mountain of the LORD's house shall be established as the highest of the mountains, and shall be raised above the hills; all the nations shall stream to it. Many peoples shall come and say, "Come, let us go up to the mountain of the LORD, to the house of the God of Jacob; that he may teach us his ways and that we may walk in his paths." For out of Zion shall go forth instruction, and the word of the LORD from Jerusalem. He shall judge between the nations, and shall arbitrate for many peoples; they shall beat their swords into plowshares, and their spears into pruning hooks; nation shall not lift up sword against nation, neither shall they learn war any more. (Isa 2:2–4)

Like many of his contemporaries, Jesus of Nazareth carried this torch, first lit by the Hebrew prophets, into the Roman world. He too imagined a Day when all would be set right. But in the wake of his crucifixion, the first Christians began to subtly reshape this vision. Jesus hope for *YHWH's intervention* in history quickly became the church's hope for *Jesus' intervention* in history. Jesus' anticipation of *YHWH's apocalypse* was transfigured into the anticipation of *Jesus' apocalypse*.

A REVELATORY VISION AT PATMOS

The spread of the burgeoning Christian movement across the Mediterranean often went hand-in-hand with the domestication of its wilder speculative edges. The immanent expectation of Jesus' return, exemplified by Paul's earliest preaching (see, e.g., 1 Thess 4:13—5:11), is quickly replaced by exhortations to marry, get a job, and avoid disturbing one's neighbors—not to mention the imperial authorities (see, e.g., Rom 13:1–7). Under the theological language of cessationism, the charismatic gifts common among the first Christian converts—visions, healing, prophecy, speaking angelic languages—are sealed into an archaic past. The radical angelology and cosmological speculation of the Palestinian church—exemplified by Jude and 2 Peter—is decentered by the exile of Judeans following the First Jewish–Roman War of 66–74 CE. But if it is domesticated, scattered, and decentered, this radical edge never disappears entirely. Its persistence is in no small part because this imaginative theology maintains a key foothold within the biblical canon, through the apocalyptic visions of a man named John of Patmos.

While traditionally conflated with John son of Zebedee, one of the twelve apostles, critical consensus now overwhelmingly agrees that John of Patmos was a second- or third-generation Christian. Little is definitively known about this enigmatic figure, other than that he appears to have been a self-styled Jewish-Christian prophet. But despite this admittedly sketchy biography, John remains central to the shape of apocalyptically minded Christianity for one simple reason: his text would become the final book of the Christian canon—Revelation.

In this masterwork, John records a series of explosive visions while facing exile on the island of Patmos. There, he says, he was "in the spirit" (Rev 1:10). John is undergoing an ecstatic experience—a fact anyone familiar with the almost psychedelic nature of the text can easily affirm. Angels, monsters, demons, comets, the sun turned to blood; this vision stitches together stock imagery from across the Jewish prophetic tradition with an imminent expectation of Jesus' return. The result is *the* classic example of apocalyptic literature within Christianity.

Apocalyptic literature (from the Greek *apokalypsis*, "to unveil") is a genre of Jewish prophetic writing epitomized by a visionary journey into the heavenly realm—often accompanied by an angelic tour guide. While, in contemporary parlance, "apocalypse" generally means "destruction" or "the end of the world"—whether of the zombie or asteroid flavor—within Jewish literature, apocalypse refers instead to a dramatic shift to a cosmic perspective. These texts generally narrate an ecstatic experience (a vision, dream, or other rapturous state) through which a prophet is granted access to the unfolding development of history from a divine perspective. Apocalyptic literature often exhibits an eschatological dualism, distinguishing between the present evil age and a coming age characterized by justice and peace.

Popular throughout the Second Temple period immediately preceding the composition of the New Testament, this literature makes only a few appearances in the biblical canon. Examples of biblical apocalyptic literature include the second half of the book of Daniel, portions of Isaiah, and scattered passages throughout the New Testament, such as Jesus' proclamations of the imminent destruction of the temple (Mark 13). Outside of the Western biblical canon, texts such as *1 Enoch* and *Jubilees* (which played a prominent role in chapter 2) are clear examples of this literary genre. But it is only in Revelation that we have a complete example of apocalyptic literature within the Western biblical canon.

LIVING UNDER EMPIRE

The internal structure of John's vision is famously difficult to map. Marked by literary allusions to the Hebrew Scriptures, numerological symbolism, and nonlinear storytelling, scholars—both amateur and professional—have sought in vain to systematize this intricate narrative. Nevertheless, despite these difficulties, the basic shape of the narrative can be presented (albeit in an oversimplified form) in four major sections.

In the first section (chapters 1–3), John enters into a visionary state and transcribes seven letters to Christian churches across Asia Minor—that is, modern-day Turkey. These letters are dictated by the Son of Man, Jesus the Christ. Here, Jesus is presented through layers of symbolic detail:

> Clothed with a long robe and with a golden sash across his chest. His head and his hair were white as white wool, white as snow; his eyes were like a flame of fire; his feet were like burnished bronze, refined as in a furnace, and his voice was like the sound of many waters. In his right hand he held seven stars, and from his mouth came a sharp, two-edged sword, and his face was like the sun shining with full force. (Rev 1:13–16)

Each of these seven short letters address both real-world concerns among the early Christian movement and point towards recurring difficulties of faithful life under empire in any era. In this way, Revelation seeks to address the question: how can the Christian community maintain loyalty, faith, and hope in the midst of a world contented by economic prosperity and blind to the violence that supports it?

THE LION AND THE LAMB

Following these seven introductory letters, the narrative quickly shifts to its second major section, a grand theophany (Rev 4–5). Here, John of Patmos crosses the threshold into the divine throne room. Borrowing images from Isaiah and Ezekiel, John describes a powerful vision of YHWH seated on a majestic throne. On this seat of power, the ancient of days is accompanied by an impressive retinue of twenty-four enthroned elders—presumably, from John's Jewish-Christian perspective, these would comprise both the twelve tribes of Israel and the twelve apostles. Together with these elders, YHWH is flanked by four monstrous angelic beings, employing imagery from both Isaiah's seraphim and Ezekiel's cherubim. These four "living beings" circle the throne of YHWH, eternally chanting: "Holy, holy, holy is the LORD God the Almighty, who was and is and is to come" (Rev 4:8).

In the midst of this overwhelming experience, YHWH reveals to the assembled divine court a scroll that seems poised to unveil and enact genuine divine justice in a world of injustice. But awe quickly turns to mourning, as it is discovered that "no one in heaven or on earth or under the earth was able to open the scroll or to look into it" (Rev 5:3).

Hope is not lost, though. John is soon informed by one of the twenty-four elders that there is in fact one who can open the scroll, the great lion of Judah. Here, in the first great reversal of the text, John turns around to view this ferocious lion, only to be met by a lamb standing before him stained with blood, its throat cut. This lamb has been sacrificed. The Christian imagery is unmistakable. This sacrificial lamb is the crucified Jesus. A ferocious victor who can overcome evil has come, but paradoxically, victory looks an awful lot like defeat.

SEALS, TRUMPETS, AND BOWLS

The third major section of the text begins with the lamb breaking the first seal of this divine scroll, thereby kicking off a Matryoshka doll of nested judgments (Rev 6–19). First, the seven seals that secure the scroll are broken—seven being a symbolically significant number representing divine completeness (think of the seven days of creation). With the breaking of the seventh seal, seven trumpets are given to the angels, each to be blown in turn. With the blast of the seventh trumpet, seven bowls of judgment are subsequently poured out.

This central section of the text provides most of the imagery associated with the book of Revelation. Fire and brimstone, earthquakes and thunder; Death mounted on horseback and the sun turned to blood; terrifying creatures emerging from bottomless pits and archangelic warriors battling dragons; even the infamous coded symbol 666—all appear in these central chapters. To describe this book as cinematographic would be an understatement. But it is important not to lose the forest for the trees. While there is certainly much of theological significance to be gleaned from a careful study of each of these images, what is more significant is the overarching structure.

For, despite its dark atmosphere and chaotic imagery, Revelation is a book about hope. YHWH has seen the suffering of those living under empire, has seen what the spirit of Babylon has done to this world, and refuses to sit on the sidelines. Revelation is not written to the comfortable or the wealthy. It is not written to a middle-class suburban church. Revelation is a letter of hope to the underclasses, the victims of empire, the subaltern.

And so, in the culminating moments of this section, the fall of empire is announced from the heavens with these triumphant words:

> Fallen, fallen is Babylon the great! It has become a dwelling place of demons, a haunt of every foul spirit, a haunt of every foul bird, a haunt of every foul and hateful beast. For all the nations have drunk of the wine of the wrath of her fornication, and the kings of the earth have committed fornication with her, and the merchants of the earth have grown rich from the power of her luxury. (Rev 18:2–3)

Here, Babylon is presented as both a spiritual evil and an all-too-human empire. Babylon provides shelter for the corruption of evil spirits and the violence of kings; the monstrosity of beasts and the economic injustice of merchants. As above, so below.

In one particularly poignant example of divine justice, at the breaking of the sixth seal, the world is struck by a great earthquake. The moon turns to blood and the stars fall from the sky. It's a scene from a '90s disaster movie. In the midst of this cosmic upheaval, John describes the panic of those on the earth who flee for safety:

> Then the kings of the earth and the magnates and the generals and the rich and the powerful and everyone, slave and free, hid in the caves and among the rocks of the mountains, calling to the mountains and rocks, "Fall on us and hide us from the face of the one seated on the throne and from the wrath of the Lamb, for the great day of their wrath has come, and who is able to stand?" (Rev 6:15–17)

Here, as the earth trembles and the stars fall—as the goodness of creation reverses itself into primordial chaos—the kings and magnates, the generals and the rich find themselves tucked away in the very same caves, side-by-side with slaves. The cosmic leveling of mountains points to a social leveling of equally cosmic proportions. Their money, power, and authority has come to naught. In the face of divine justice, it means nothing.

This is the promise of Revelation: Every power that views itself as eternal is ultimately finite. All suffering and every injustice eventually comes to an end. Violence and death will not have the final say. Indeed, even death itself is cast into a lake of fire to be burned away (Rev 20:14). Revelation is the revolutionary literature that gives all who have been crushed by the empire hope to see that empire's end. At a time when unprecedented prosperity has been paired with unprecedented inequality and suffering, those of us on the imperial core should heed this warning.

A NEW HEAVEN AND A NEW EARTH

In the wake of these twenty-one judgments (seven seals + seven trumpets + seven bowls), John's vision comes to its climax in a final major section (Rev 19–22). In the heavens, the assembled martyrs, elders, and angelic beings erupt into spontaneous praise for the victory of YHWH over the spiritual and material forces of evil and injustice. Meanwhile, on the earth, the penultimate confrontation between YHWH and Babylon is prepared.

At this conflict, the Son of Man, mounted on horseback, descends from the heavens, covered in blood and leading an army to crush Babylon for good. Here, we have the culmination of messianic anticipation; the advent of a salvific redeemer ready to pounce on evil like a lion. Specifically, John evokes the shockingly violent imagery of Isaiah 63—a disturbing vision of the divine stomping the citizens of Edom to death in a winepress, popping their broken bodies like grapes.

But something strange is going on here. The text is littered with small inconsistencies that don't quite add up. The Son of Man is descending from the heavens toward a cosmic battle in a bloody robe. But if he's descending toward the confrontation, then why are his clothes already bloody before the combat has even begun? Or, put another way, whose blood is on his robes? It is his own. This is not the image of a bloodthirsty messiah, but of a slain victor; not a lion, but a sacrificial lamb. In the same way, this victorious figure carries a sword. But where is this sword? It is not in his hand, ready to strike and kill; the sword is in his mouth. Indeed, this "sword" is no sword at all it is the words of judgment against violence and death. Finally, the Son of Man is described as leading a great army. But who composes this army? Not soldiers, but martyrs. It is an army not of those who bring death, but of those who have received it. Just as in the theophanic throne-room scene at the opening of the seals, John has instituted a series of unexpected reversals. In his deft literary hand and visionary mind, these grotesque images of violence and death have been turned upside down, transfigured into images of the hope for the end of death and violence. Victory is won, not by employing the methods of Babylon, but by subverting them. "The master's tools," Audre Lorde famously remarked, "will never dismantle the master's house."[1]

In the wake of this victory, the Son of Man institutes a thousand-year reign. An angelic being binds the satan—a divine being who represents the spiritual and material forces of Babylon—and casts him into a bottomless pit to await his final verdict while the martyred faithful sit in judgment over the nations, ruling together with Christ. This, we are told, is "the first resurrection" (Rev 20:6).

After this thousand-year interlude, the satan is released for the final climactic confrontation. His forces encircle the ruling saints but are summarily destroyed by a fire from the heavens. The satan himself is cast into the now infamous "lake of fire," where he is consumed. The dead then arise and assemble before the throne for judgment. Those found in the Book of Life are welcomed into the dawning kingdom of resurrected life, while their oppressors are cast into the lake of fire. This is not the "eternal torment" you heard about in Sunday school. In John's cosmic vision the tools of Babylon—oppression, Death, and even Hades itself—are annihilated in the lake of fire (Rev 20:14). Having overcome the spirit of Babylon that enslaved the nations, the heavenly Jerusalem has stripped it of its only powers. And so, with this final resurrection of the faithful and destruction of Babylon and Death, justice overcomes injustice, peace overcomes war, and life overcomes death.

NEW JERUSALEM, NEW EDEN

Despite this violence, Revelation is not primarily preoccupied with the negativity of death—even the death of death—but with the constructive power of life. And so, the fall of Babylon dialectically sublates itself into a renewal of all creation: "then I saw a new heaven and a new earth, for the first heaven and the first earth had passed away" (Rev 21:1). The closing chapters of Revelation narrate the birth of this new kingdom of peace and justice through the emergence of the New Jerusalem, a city that descends from the heavens to establish the reign of YHWH on earth. Borrowing nuptial metaphors from the Hebrew Scriptures, John employs vivid bridal imagery to encapsulate this most joyous occasion. For Jeremiah, there will be no need for an ark of the covenant, because all of Jerusalem shall be the

---

1. Lorde, *The Master's Tools Will Never Dismantle the Master's House*.

throne of YHWH, and the nations from all the earth will stream to it (Jer 3:16). Indeed, "Its gates will never be shut" (Rev 21:25). John takes this logic one step further. Not only will there be no ark, there will be no temple; for all of the New Jerusalem, indeed the whole cosmos, will be the temple to the glory of YHWH. Just as in Genesis 1, all of creation has become the dwelling place of the presence of YHWH's life-giving energy. There is no temple in the New Jerusalem for precisely the same reason that there was no temple in the first Eden, because the glory is not confined to one room or one building; it saturates everything.

In case this connection wasn't obvious enough, at the center of the New Jerusalem, John places the tree of life, beside which flow rivers of divine life-giving water. On this renewed holy mountain, YHWH's life-giving energy flows freely through the center of the city. The river is flanked on both sides by the tree of life, now gloriously imaged as one tree that nevertheless bears twelve fruits—symbolically the twelve tribes but perhaps also one for each month, so that none shall hunger. At this tree, not only have the twelve tribes of Israel been renewed, but the righteous from across the nations have been grafted into this new family tree that heals the rifts of the nations. The work to which Sarah and Abraham's family was called from the beginning (Gen 12:3) has now, in this final culminating vision, been brought to its fruition:

> Then the angel showed me the river of the water of life, bright as crystal, flowing from the throne of God and of the Lamb through the middle of the street of the city. On either side of the river is the tree of life with its twelve kinds of fruit, producing its fruit each month; and the leaves of the tree are for the healing of the nations. Nothing accursed will be found there any more. (Rev 22:1–3a)

In this way, this epic story ends where it began: on Mount Eden, saturated with the life-giving presence and energy of YHWH.

The story ends where it began, but it does not end in exactly the same way that it began. Cosmic history, according to John of Patmos, is *not* a flat circle. The grand biblical narrative that John brings to a close, and that we have sought to trace through this book, is like Joseph Campbell's "monomyth," where the hero returns deeply and irreversibly changed.[2] Here, the "hero" is nothing less than the cosmos itself. In John's concluding vision, the cosmos—both the heavens and earth—have been so radically transfigured by the love and justice of YHWH that they have functionally merged

2. Campbell, *Hero with a Thousand Faces*.

one into the other. The descent of the New Jerusalem is, in this way, the descent of the heavens themselves. All of creation has become the cosmic mountain, the place where the heavens and the earth overlap, where the gods and mere mortals cohabit.

WHAT NOW?

But we do not live on this renewed Eden. We are not on the cosmic mountain. Revelation is an anticipatory text. We need only open a newspaper to recognize that we are far from a cosmic reconciliation. We are still waiting for the Day of divine justice—indeed, we'd be happy to experience even human justice once in a while.

Apocalyptic literature is a literature of waiting. We live under the conditions of violence, oppression, and death. Babylon still reigns here. In short, we still live in exile. Everywhere that the sick are not healed, we live in exile. Everywhere the homeless are not housed, we live in exile. Everywhere that the naked are not clothed, the mourning are not comforted, and prisoners are not set free, we live in exile. But Revelation was written precisely to those who live in the conspicuous absence of the divine, who suffer under injustice, and who seek to live faithfully in the context of empire.

Revelation is a book of waiting, but not a passive waiting. Our task is not to fret over times and dates, like those preachers who, every six months or so, predict the return of Jesus. As he himself remarked, "about that day and hour no one knows, neither the angels of heaven, nor the Son, but only the Father" (Matt 24:36). Instead of passivity, Revelation encourages an active, hopeful waiting.

The renewed Eden isn't a literal mountain. You can't visit it; you can't have a picnic at its base. You can't scale its peak or buy a T-shirt at its gift shop. Eden is a myth. But even so, it offers us encouragement and hope. Hope that justice overcomes injustice, that peace overcomes war, that life overcomes death. Eden reminds us that empire doesn't have the last word, that Babylon doesn't win. And so, in a way, in the midst of exile, we are tasked with ascending this mythical mountain, seeking and searching for the reconciliation of the nations and the renewal of all things. Even if we know we will never quite reach that peak, we can hope and we can wait expectantly; saying, "Come, let us go up to the mountain of the LORD, to the house of the God of Jacob; that he may teach us his ways and that we may walk in his paths" (Isa 2:3).

Study Guide

CHAPTER 1—EDEN: THE MOUNTAIN OF CO-CREATION

Prayer

> O LORD, our Sovereign,
>   how majestic is your name in all the earth!
> You have set your glory above the heavens.
>   Out of the mouths of babes and infants
> you have founded a bulwark because of your foes,
>   to silence the enemy and the avenger.
> When I look at your heavens, the work of your fingers,
>   the moon and the stars that you have established;
> what are humans that you are mindful of them,
>   mortals that you care for them?
> Yet you have made them a little lower than God
>   and crowned them with glory and honor.
> You have given them dominion over the works of your hands;
>   you have put all things under their feet,
> all sheep and oxen,
>   and also the beasts of the field,
> the birds of the air, and the fish of the sea,
>   whatever passes along the paths of the seas.
> O LORD, our Sovereign,
>   how majestic is your name in all the earth!
> (Psalm 8)

Study Guide

Suggested Scripture Readings

Genesis 1–3

Questions for Discussion/Reflection

1. The editors and compilers of Genesis 1 and 2—living in exile—claimed the whole world was a temple. Do we have the spiritual imagination today to claim that the whole world is a place of YHWH's living presence? How would we live differently if we really believed that?
2. What does it mean to be created in the image of YHWH?
3. In Genesis 2, human beings are created from a combination of dirt and divine spirit. How does this make us think about what it means to be human?
4. Genesis 2 never explicitly describes the Garden of Eden as a mountain, how might your understanding of the Eden story change if you imagine the garden as a cosmic mountain, as Ezekiel suggests?
5. Why would YHWH place a tree in the garden that you are not supposed to eat? Is the command arbitrary, pointless, even cruel?
6. In grasping for the knowledge of good and evil, Adam and Eve come to realize their separateness. In what ways is this realization necessary for the development moral consciousness? Conversely, in what ways might this realization lead to harm?

Challenge

Experience nature in a new way and think about how the divine might be present there.

Suggested Further Readings

Richard J. Clifford, *The Cosmic Mountain in Canaan and the Old Testament* (1972)
Peter Enns, *The Evolution of Adam: What the Bible Does and Doesn't Say about Human Origins* (2012)
Matthew Fox, *Original Blessing* (2000)

Cultural Engagements

Novel: C. S. Lewis, *Perelandra* (1943)
Film: Terrance Malick, director, *The Tree of Life* (2011)
Documentary: P. Northcutt and D. Kenard, directors, *Journey of the Universe* (2011)

CHAPTER 2—HERMON: THE MOUNTAIN OF COSMIC REVOLT

Prayer

> God has taken his place in the divine council;
>   in the midst of the gods he holds judgment:
> "How long will you judge unjustly
>   and show partiality to the wicked? *Selah*
> Give justice to the weak and the orphan;
>   maintain the right of the lowly and the destitute.
> Rescue the weak and the needy;
>   deliver them from the hand of the wicked."
> They have neither knowledge nor understanding;
>   they walk around in darkness;
>   all the foundations of the earth are shaken.
> I say, "You are gods,
>   children of the Most High, all of you;
> nevertheless, you shall die like mortals
>   and fall like any prince."
> Rise up, O God, judge the earth,
>   for all the nations belong to you!
> (Psalm 82)

Suggested Scripture Readings

Genesis 4–11; Deuteronomy 32; *1 Enoch* 1–9 (Note: *1 Enoch* is not in Western Bibles)

Questions for Discussion/Reflection

1. Why does YHWH accept Abel's sacrifice and not Cain's? Is YHWH bloodthirsty, demanding death in Their sacrifices?

2. The modern concept of monotheism assumes that YHWH is sitting alone in heaven. But the ancient worldview imagined a rich diversity of lesser divine beings. How does the story of YHWH's divine council and their rebellion affect the way we read the rest of the Bible?

3. In this chapter, we engage with ideas from *1 Enoch*, a book that is important to the Bible—even cited in Jude and alluded to in 1 Peter—but wasn't included in the canon of Scripture. What does it mean for a book to be "in" or "out" of the Bible? How should we think about books like *1 Enoch* that weren't included, but were nonetheless key to the shape of the Bible as we know it?

4. Why does YHWH flood the earth? Why do They destroy Their own creation?

5. We have suggested key parallels between Eve and Adam eating the fruit, divine beings rebelling, and humanity building a tower. How does reading these vastly different mythological stories together deepen their meaning and enrich your reading?

6. Humans have a choice between two ways of life: the co-creativity of Eden or the coercive power of Babel. What are the "Babels" of our world today? What structures are built to seize and maintain power?

Challenge

Find a small way to materially support disaster-relief efforts.

Suggested Further Readings

Terence E. Fretheim, *Creation Untamed: The Bible, God, and Natural Disasters* (2010)
Michael S. Heiser, *The Unseen Realm: Recovering the Supernatural Worldview of the Bible* (2015)
Michael S. Heiser, *Reversing Hermon: Enoch, the Watchers, and the Forgotten Mission of Jesus Christ* (2017)

Cultural Engagements

Novel: John Steinbeck, *East of Eden* (1952)
Film: Darren Aronofsky, director, *Noah* (2014)

CHAPTER 3—MORIAH: THE MOUNTAIN OF SACRIFICE

Prayer

> Create in me a clean heart, O God,
>   and put a new and right spirit within me.
> Do not cast me away from your presence,
>   and do not take your holy spirit from me.
> Restore to me the joy of your salvation,
>   and sustain in me a willing spirit.
>
> Then I will teach transgressors your ways,
>   and sinners will return to you.
> Deliver me from bloodshed, O God,
>   O God of my salvation,
>   and my tongue will sing aloud of your deliverance.
>
> O LORD, open my lips,
>   and my mouth will declare your praise.
> For you have no delight in sacrifice;
>   if I were to give a burnt offering, you would not be pleased.
> The sacrifice acceptable to God is a broken spirit;
>   a broken and contrite heart, O God, you will not despise.
>
> Do good to Zion in your good pleasure;
>   rebuild the walls of Jerusalem;
> then you will delight in right sacrifices,
>   in burnt offerings and whole burnt offerings;
>   then bulls will be offered on your altar.
>
> (Psalm 51:10–19)

Suggested Scripture Readings

Genesis 12–22

Questions for Discussion/Reflection

1. Why does YHWH call Abraham: "Go forth from your native land and from your father's house, to the land that I will show you" (Gen 12:1–3)? If you were tasked with leaving friends and family, everything you know and love, could you do it?

2. After splitting a number of animals, Abraham falls into a deep sleep, as a flaming torch passes between the animals. What does it mean that YHWH promises to keep the covenant and Abraham doesn't?

3. Sarah gives Hagar, a slave, to Abraham for sex. Nowhere are we told that Hagar consented. Moreover, once Sarah and Abraham conceive a child of their own, they banish Hagar and her child into the wilderness to die. How do we make sense of the profound ethical failures of even the most faithful "heroes" of the Bible?

4. In what ways does our impatience lead us to violently seize control of situations, as Abraham and Sarah do with Hagar?

5. YHWH asks Abraham to perform the unthinkable: to kill his son. This is completely contrary to the way we think of YHWH's character. Was Abraham right to obey? Why was Abraham willing to sacrifice his son?

6. Abraham ascends the mountain of YHWH in order to offer the ultimate sacrifice. Yet, this is also the place from which he receives the greatest gift. In what ways are gifts accompanied by sacrifice?

Challenge

Find the most sentimentally valuable object you are willing to part with and give it to someone as a gift.

Suggested Further Readings

Delores Williams, *Sisters in the Wilderness: The Challenge of Womanist God-Talk* (2013)
Søren Kierkegaard, *Fear and Trembling* (1843; Hong translation, 1983)
Jacques Derrida, *The Gift of Death* (1992)

Cultural Engagements

Novel: Toni Morrison, *Beloved* (2004)
Film: Andrei Tarkovsky, director, *The Sacrifice* (1986)

CHAPTER 4—SINAI: THE MOUNTAIN OF COVENANT

Prayer

> I will sing to the LORD, for he has triumphed gloriously;
>   horse and rider he has thrown into the sea.
> The LORD is my strength and my might,
>   and he has become my salvation;
> this is my God, and I will praise him;
>   my father's God, and I will exalt him.
> The LORD is a warrior;
>   the LORD is his name.
> Pharaoh's chariots and his army he cast into the sea;
>   his elite officers were sunk in the Red Sea.
> The floods covered them;
>   they went down into the depths like a stone.
> Your right hand, O LORD, glorious in power—
>   your right hand, O LORD, shattered the enemy.
> In the greatness of your majesty you overthrew your adversaries;
>   you sent out your fury; it consumed them like stubble.
> At the blast of your nostrils the waters piled up;
>   the floods stood up in a heap;
>   the deeps congealed in the heart of the sea.
> The enemy said, "I will pursue; I will overtake;
>   I will divide the spoil; my desire shall have its fill of them.
>   I will draw my sword; my hand shall destroy them."
> You blew with your wind; the sea covered them;
>   they sank like lead in the mighty waters.
> Who is like you, O LORD, among the gods?
>   Who is like you, majestic in holiness,
>   awesome in splendor, doing wonders?
> You stretched out your right hand;
>   the earth swallowed them.
>
> (Exodus 15:1–12)

Suggested Scripture Readings

Exodus 1–5; 12–14; 19–20; 24–26; 40

Study Guide

Questions for Discussion/Reflection

1. Exodus portrays Egypt as an exemplar of the destructive spirit of Babylon. What characteristics mark this spirit? Where do we see this spirit today?
2. The first half of Exodus is the narrative of YHWH's liberating the Hebrews from slavery in Egypt. Why does YHWH side with the Hebrews against the Egyptians?
3. As he approaches the burning bush, Moses is told that he is on "holy ground" and must remove his sandals (Exod 3:5). What does it mean to be on holy ground and why does that require removing sandals?
4. At the culmination of the plagues, YHWH kills the firstborn sons of all the families of Egypt. How do we reconcile this act with our understanding of YHWH as loving and just?
5. As they approach Mount Sinai, the Hebrews are told to "be careful not to go up to the mountain or to touch the edge of it, any who touches the mountain shall be put to death" (Exod 19:12). Why is Sinai so dangerous? How does imagining YHWH as dangerous change the way you think about the life of faith?
6. The Hebrews are rescued for the purpose of worshiping YHWH on the mountain, but when they arrive, YHWH develops a plan to leave the mountain temple and join the people in a mobile tabernacle. Why not stay on the mountain?

Challenge

Do something that feels dangerous.

Suggested Further Readings

Rudolf Otto, *The Idea of the Holy* (1923)
James H. Cone, *God of the Oppressed* (1975)
Angeline M. G. Song, *A Postcolonial Woman's Encounter with Moses and Miriam* (2015)

Cultural Engagements

Novel: Herman Melville, *Moby-Dick* (1851)
Film: Ridley Scott, director, *Exodus: Gods and Kings* (2014)

CHAPTER 5—ZION: THE MOUNTAIN OF DIVINE DWELLING

Prayer

> How lovely is your dwelling place,
>   O LORD of hosts!
> My soul longs, indeed it faints,
>   for the courts of the LORD;
> my heart and my flesh sing for joy
>   to the living God.
> Even the sparrow finds a home
>   and the swallow a nest for herself,
>   where she may lay her young,
> at your altars, O LORD of hosts,
>   my King and my God.
> Happy are those who live in your house,
>   ever singing your praise. *Selah*
> Happy are those whose strength is in you,
>   in whose heart are the highways to Zion.
> As they go through the valley of Baca,
>   they make it a place of springs;
>   the early rain also covers it with pools.
> They go from strength to strength;
>   the God of gods will be seen in Zion.
> (Psalm 84:1–7)

Suggested Scripture Readings

1 Samuel 8; 15–16; 2 Samuel 7; 11; Deuteronomy 17:14–20; 1 Kings 8; 11–12

Questions for Discussion/Reflection

1. In 1 Samuel 8, the people of Israel demand a king like the other nations. Why is it problematic for Israel to want a king?
2. When David proposes to build a temple on Mount Zion, YHWH initially refuses. Why is YHWH hesitant about the temple?
3. What is the theological significance of the difference between a mobile tabernacle and a stationary temple?
4. David is called "a man after the LORD's own heart" (1 Sam 13:14), but he is also guilty of rape and murder. How do we reconcile this?
5. Compare the Torah regulations for kings (Deut 17:14–20) with the opening narratives of Solomon's reign (1 Kgs 11–12). How does Solomon measure up to the Deuteronomic ideal?
6. All of the Davidic kings have ambiguous reigns. In what ways do the reigns of David, Solomon, Rehoboam recapitulate the destructive spirit of Babylon?

Challenge

Select three to five objects and make an altar to YHWH.

Suggested Further Readings

Margaret Barker, *Temple Theology: An Introduction* (2004)
Walter Brueggemann, *Chosen? Reading the Bible amid the Israeli-Palestinian Conflict* (2015)
Mitri Raheb, *Decolonizing Palestine: The Land, the People, the Bible* (2023)

Cultural Engagements

Novel: Terry Prachett, *Small Gods* (2013)
Film: Ridley Scott, director, *Kingdom of Heaven: Director's Cut* (2005)

CHAPTER 6—HOREB: THE MOUNTAIN OF SACRED SILENCE

Prayer

> By the rivers of Babylon—
>> there we sat down, and there we wept
>> when we remembered Zion.
>
> On the willows there
>> we hung up our harps.
>
> For there our captors
>> asked us for songs,
>
> and our tormentors asked for mirth, saying,
>> "Sing us one of the songs of Zion!"
>
> How could we sing the LORD's song
>> in a foreign land?
>
> If I forget you, O Jerusalem,
>> let my right hand wither!
>
> Let my tongue cling to the roof of my mouth,
>> if I do not remember you,
>
> if I do not set Jerusalem
>> above my highest joy.
>
> (Psalm 137:1-6)

Suggested Scripture Readings

Amos 5; 1 Kings 18:16-42; 19:1—18; 2 Kings 24-25; Ezekiel 10

Questions for Discussion/Reflection

1. Elijah expects to find YHWH in the loud and intense experiences of wind, earthquake, and fire. Instead, he encounters YHWH in a still small voice. How might loud, bombastic, and exciting experiences mask the silence of YHWH?

2. In contemporary Western Christianity, we tend to think of YHWH as the only god, fully distinct from all other beings. But in many biblical texts—such as 1 Kings 18—we see YHWH in open combat with other gods, such as Baal. What do we do with such texts, which rely on a radically different understanding of the spiritual world?

3. In Amos 5:21–24, YHWH rejects songs, festivals, and prayers in favor of justice. How might the smells and bells—or smoke machines and worship bands—of the church mask deeper structures of injustice?

4. The Babylonian king, Nebuchadnezzar, destroyed Jerusalem and the temple of YHWH on Mount Zion. Why is this theologically significant?

5. As the Babylonian army sweeps through Jerusalem, Ezekiel envisions YHWH leaving the temple to its destruction. How do we make sense of YHWH abandoning Their people to be exiled and the temple destroyed?

6. How do we differentiate between Elijah's experience of YHWH in the silence, and Ezekiel's experience of the silence of YHWH? What are examples of each of these experiences from your own life?

Challenge

Abandon the comforts of home and travel farther by foot, bike, or wheelchair than you ever have before.

Suggested Further Readings

Walter Brueggemann, *The Prophetic Imagination*, 40th anniversary ed. (2018; original, 1978).
James L. Kugel, *The Great Shift: Encountering God in the Biblical Era* (2017)
Richard Rubenstein, *After Auschwitz: Radical Theology and Contemporary Judaism* (1966)

Cultural Engagements

Novel: Shūsaku Endō, *Silence: A Novel* (1966)
Film: Andy De Emmony, director, *God on Trial* (2008)

CHAPTER 7—TABOR: THE MOUNTAIN OF UNVEILING

Prayer

> The LORD says to my lord,
>   "Sit at my right hand

until I make your enemies your footstool."
The LORD sends out from Zion
   your mighty scepter.
   Rule in the midst of your foes.
Your people will offer themselves willingly
   on the day you lead your forces
   on the holy mountains.
From the womb of the morning,
   like dew, your youth will come to you.
The LORD has sworn and will not change his mind,
   "You are a priest forever according to the order of Melchizedek."
The LORD is at your right hand;
   he will shatter kings on the day of his wrath.
He will execute judgment among the nations,
   filling them with corpses;
he will shatter heads
   over the wide earth.
He will drink from the stream by the path;
   therefore he will lift up his head.
(Psalm 110)

Suggested Scripture Readings

Ezra 3; Mark 1–10

Questions for Discussion/Reflection

1. Why do the "old people who had seen the first house on its foundations" weep at the construction of the second temple, while the young sing? (Ezra 3:10–13) Why didn't the glory return to the second temple?

2. In Mark 1:14, Jesus announces the arrival of the reign of YHWH. While often confused with heaven, Jesus has a much more grounded account of the reign of YHWH. What does he mean by the reign of YHWH?

3. The Gospel of Mark consistently uses the patriarchal language of "king" and "kingdom." From a contemporary perspective, to what extent does this capture or obscure Jesus' mission?

4. Why do the scribes find it offensive, or even blasphemous, for Jesus to say "your sins are forgiven" (Mark 2:5–7)?

5. In Mark 9:3, Jesus' clothing shines a "dazzling white," signifying the presence of the glory of YHWH. What does it mean to think of Jesus, a first-century itinerant preacher, as bearing the glory of YHWH into the world?

6. Why does Peter desire to build tents on the top of the transfiguration mountain (Mark 9:5)? Why does Jesus say "no"?

Challenge

Meditate on the light of a fire, whether from a candle or a bonfire.

Suggested Further Readings

Daniel Boyarin, *The Jewish Gospels: The Story of the Jewish Christ* (2013)
Bart D. Ehrman, *How Jesus Became God: The Exaltation of the Jewish Preacher from Galilee* (2015)
Kelly Brown Douglas, *The Black Christ* (1993)

Cultural Engagements

Novel: Friedrich Nietzsche, "Thus Spoke Zarathustra" (1883–85) in *The Portable Nietzsche* (1977)
Film: Terry Jones, director, *Monty Python's The Life of Brian* (1979)
Musical: David Greene, director, *Godspell* (1973)

CHAPTER 8—GOLGOTHA: THE MOUNTAIN OF DEATH

Prayer

> My God, my God, why have you forsaken me?
>   Why are you so far from helping me, from the words of my groaning?
> O my God, I cry by day, but you do not answer;
>   and by night but find no rest.
> I am poured out like water,
>   and all my bones are out of joint;
> my heart is like wax;
>   it is melted within my breast;

> my mouth is dried up like a potsherd,
> > and my tongue sticks to my jaws;
> > you lay me in the dust of death.
> For dogs are all around me;
> > a company of evildoers encircles me;
> they bound my hands and feet.
> I can count all my bones.
> They stare and gloat over me;
> they divide my clothes among themselves,
> > and for my clothing they cast lots.
> But you, O LORD, do not be far away!
> > O my help, come quickly to my aid!
> Deliver my soul from the sword,
> > my life from the power of the dog!
> (Psalm 22:1–2, 14–20)

Suggested Scripture Readings

Mark 11:1—16:8

Questions for Discussion/Reflection

1. As Jesus enters Jerusalem (Mark 11:1–11), the crowds chant "Hosanna! Blessed is the one who comes in the name of the LORD! Blessed is the coming kingdom of our ancestor David! Hosanna in the highest heaven!" Why are they evoking David? What does this specific song signify?

2. Throughout the closing chapters of Mark, Jesus' critique of the temple is unrelenting: he compares the temple to a fruitless fig tree, he overturns the tables in the outer court, he preaches parables against the religious authorities, he prophesies the temple's destruction. Why does Jesus see an attack on the temple as central to his mission?

3. Why is Jesus sentenced to death? What does the *political context* of Jesus of Nazareth's execution teach us about the *theological meaning* of Christ's death?

4. If the transfiguration on Mount Tabor taught us that Jesus is the glory of YHWH returned, then how do we make sense of Jesus' cry of dereliction: "My God My God why have you forsaken me?" (Mark 15:34)

5. Mark tells us that, at the moment Jesus dies, the curtain separating off the holy of holies is torn in two (Mark 15:37). Why is this detail significant? Why does Mark place it at this culminating moment?

6. In the oldest manuscripts of Mark, the text abruptly ends at 16:8 with the words: "and they said nothing to anyone, for they were afraid." The remaining verses appear to have been added later in order to bring the narrative to a more traditional resolution. How does your reading of Mark change if the text ends at verse 8?

Challenge

Participate in a protest or political demonstration.

Suggested Further Readings

Andrew Sung Park, *Triune Atonement: Christ's Healing for Sinners, Victims, and the Whole Creation* (2009)
James H. Cone, *The Cross and Lynching Tree* (2013)
James Alison, *On Being Liked* (2004)

Cultural Engagements

Novel: Chaim Potok, *My Name is Asher Lev* (2003)
Film: John Michael McDonagh, director, *Calvary* (2014)
Musical: Norman Jewison, director, *Jesus Christ Superstar* (1973)

CHAPTER 9—OLIVET: THE MOUNTAIN OF ABSENCE

Prayer

> Then afterward
>   I will pour out my spirit on all flesh;
> your sons and your daughters shall prophesy,
>   your old men shall dream dreams,
>   and your young men shall see visions.
> Even on the male and female slaves,
>   in those days I will pour out my spirit.

> I will show portents in the heavens and on the earth, blood and fire and columns of smoke. The sun shall be turned to darkness and the moon to blood, before the great and terrible day of the LORD comes. Then everyone who calls on the name of the LORD shall be saved, for in Mount Zion and in Jerusalem there shall be those who escape, as the LORD has said, and among the survivors shall be those whom the LORD calls.
> (Joel 2:28–32)

Suggested Scripture Readings

Luke 24; Acts 1–2; 10; 15; 1 Corinthians 15; Galatians 1–4

Questions for Discussion/Reflection

1. Why is the resurrected Christ initially hidden to the disciples on the road to Emmaus? Why does he appear only at the breaking of the bread?

2. Paul describes Christ as the "first fruits of the resurrection." What does this say about Paul's understanding of Jesus' resurrection? What is the "full harvest" Paul is anticipating?

3. The resurrected Christ appears only briefly to a few of his disciples before ascending to the heavens. If the whole narrative of the Bible is about YHWH dwelling among people, why doesn't Jesus want to stay?

4. After the resurrection, Jesus tasks his followers with being his witnesses in the world, just as "a cloud took him out of their sight" (Acts 1:9). What does it look like to put the reign of YHWH into action in the absence of Christ?

5. On the day of Pentecost, people from all over the world were able to speak to one another and "each one heard them speaking in their native language" (Acts 2:6). What is the theological significance of the spirit of YHWH manifesting in this way?

6. Martin Luther King Jr. famously described 11:00 a.m. Sunday as one of the most segregated hours in Christian America. How might the early church's response to the Judaizer controversy help us deal with

contemporary forms of exclusion—including racial, sexual, and religious discrimination?

Challenge

Meditate on the absence of YHWH.

Suggested Further Readings

Robert B. Stewart, ed., *The Resurrection of Jesus: John Dominic Crossan and N. T. Wright in Dialogue* (2005)
Paula Frederiksen, *Paul: The Pagan's Apostle* (2018)
Thomas J. J. Altizer, *The Self-Embodiment of God* (1977)

Cultural Engagements

Novel: Octavia Butler, *Parable of the Sower* (1993)
Film: Ingar Bergman, director, *The Seventh Seal* (1957)

CHAPTER 10—THE NEW EDEN: THE MOUNTAIN OF RE-CREATION

Prayer

> And I heard a loud voice from the throne saying,
> "See, the home of God is among mortals.
> He will dwell with them;
> they will be his peoples,
> and God himself will be with them and be their God;
> he will wipe every tear from their eyes.
> Death will be no more;
> mourning and crying and pain will be no more,
> for the first things have passed away."
> (Revelation 21:3–4)

Suggested Scripture Readings

Isaiah 2:1–5; Micah 4; Revelation 18–22

Questions for Discussion/Reflection

1. In Isaiah 2:1–5 and Micah 4, the prophets anticipate the end of every exile. What is the significance of the mountain imagery in their visions?
2. In Revelation 19, the rider on the white horse arrives to the battle covered in blood and carrying a sword. But he is covered in blood before encountering enemies and the sword is in his mouth, not his hands. What do these small details mean? How might they influence the way we read this uncomfortable text?
3. According to Revelation 21–22, where is the ultimate destination of humanity?
4. In Revelation 21:22, John specifically notes that there is no temple in the New Jerusalem. Why is a temple no longer necessary?
5. The New Jerusalem is described as surrounded by a tall wall. Yet, we are also told that its gate is never closed. How might this evoke Isaiah's vision of all nations streaming to Zion? What might it say about contemporary politics of walls and immigration?
6. The descent of the heavenly Jerusalem in Revelation 21–22 is full of rich imagery—temple, tree of life, garden, fruit, rivers, wedding, mountains, angels, gates—what is this imagery intended to evoke?

Challenge

Return to the spot in nature where you had your week 1 reflection and attend to the echoes of YHWH's presence there.

Suggested Further Readings

Michael J. Gorman, *Reading Revelation Responsibly: Uncivil Worship and Witness: Following the Lamb into the New Creation* (2010)

N. T. Wright, *Surprised by Hope: Rethinking Heaven, the Resurrection, and the Mission of the Church* (2018)

Rita Nakashima Brock and Rebecca Ann Parker, *Saving Paradise: How Christianity Traded Love of This World for Crucifixion and Empire* (2008)

Study Guide

Cultural Engagements

Text: William Blake, *The Marriage of Heaven and Hell* (1790)
Film: Vincent Ward, director, *What Dreams May Come* (1998)
TV miniseries: Alex Garland, writer, *Devs* (2020)

Bibliography

Alison, James. *On Being Liked*. New York: Herder & Herder, 2004.
Altizer, Thomas J. J. *The New Gospel of Christian Atheism*. Aurora: Davies Group, 2002.
———. *The Self-Embodiment of God*. New York: Harper & Row, 1977.
Badiou, Alain. *Saint Paul: The Foundation of Universalism*. Translated by Ray Brassier. Stanford: Stanford University Press, 2003.
Barker, Margaret. *Temple Theology: An Introduction*. London: SPCK, 2004.
Barth, Karl. *Church Dogmatics*. Vol. II/2. 1957. Reprint, London: T&T Clark, 2010.
Blake, William. *The Marriage of Heaven and Hell*. 1790. Reprint, New York: Dover, 2013.
Borg, Marcus J., and John Dominic Crossan. *The Last Week: What the Gospels Really Teach About Jesus's Final Days in Jerusalem*. San Francisco: HarperOne, 2007.
Boyarin, Daniel. *The Jewish Gospels: The Story of the Jewish Christ*. New York: New, 2013.
Brock, Rita Nakashima, and Rebecca Ann Parker. *Saving Paradise: How Christianity Traded Love of This World for Crucifixion and Empire*. Boston: Beacon, 2008.
Brueggemann, Walter. *Chosen? Reading the Bible amid the Israeli-Palestinian Conflict*. Louisville: Westminster John Knox, 2015.
———. *The Prophetic Imagination*. 40th anniversary ed. Minneapolis: Fortress, 2018.
Bultmann, Rudolf. *Jesus Christ and Mythology*. London: SCM, 1958.
Butler, Octavia. *Parable of the Sower*. New York: Doubleday, 1993.
Campbell, Joseph. *The Hero with a Thousand Faces*. Novato, CA: New World Library, 2008.
Clifford, Richard J. *The Cosmic Mountain in Canaan and the Old Testament*. 1972. Reprint, Eugene, OR: Wipf & Stock, 2010.
Cone, James H. *The Cross and Lynching Tree*. New York: Orbis, 2013.
———. *God of the Oppressed*. New York: Orbis, 1975.
Crossan, John Dominic. *Who Killed Jesus? Exposing the Roots of Anti-Semitism in the Gospel Story of the Death of Jesus*. San Francisco: HarperCollins, 1996.
Derrida, Jacques. *The Gift of Death*. Translated by David Wills. 1992. Reprint, Chicago: University of Chicago Press, 1996.
Douglas, Kelly Brown. *The Black Christ*. New York: Orbis, 1993.
Ehrman, Bart D. *How Jesus Became God: The Exaltation of a Jewish Preacher from Galilee*. San Francisco: HarperOne, 2015.
Eiesland, Nancy L. *The Disabled God: Toward a Liberatory Theology of Disability*. Nashville: Abingdon, 1994.
Endō, Shūsaku. *Silence: A Novel*. New York: Picador Modern Classics, 2016.
Enns, Peter. *The Evolution of Adam: What the Bible Does and Doesn't Say About Human Origins*. Grand Rapids: Brazos, 2012.

Bibliography

Fox, Matthew. *Original Blessing*. New York: TarcherPerigee, 2000.
Frederiksen, Paula. *Paul: The Pagan's Apostle*. New Haven: Yale University Press, 2018.
Fretheim, Terence E. *Creation Untamed: The Bible, God, and Natural Disasters*. Grand Rapids: Baker Academic, 2010.
Gorman, Michael J. *Reading Revelation Responsibly: Uncivil Worship and Witness: Following the Lamb into the New Creation*. Eugene, OR: Cascade, 2010.
Hartke, Austin. *Transforming: The Bible and the Lives of Transgender Christians*. Louisville: Westminster John Knox, 2018.
Heiser, Michael S. "Deuteronomy 32:8 and the Sons of God." *Bibliotheca Sacra* 158 (2001) 52–74.
———. *Reversing Hermon: Enoch, the Watchers, and the Forgotten Mission of Jesus Christ*. Crane, MO: Defender, 2017.
———. *The Unseen Realm: Rediscovering the Supernatural Worldview of the Bible*. Bellingham, WA: Lexham, 2015.
Homer. *The Iliad with an English Translation*. Translated by A. T. Murray. Cambridge: Harvard University Press, 1924.
———. *Odyssey*. Translated by Stanley Lombardo. Cambridge: Hackett Classics, 2000.
Hoppin, Ruth. *Priscilla's Letter: Finding the Author of the Epistle to the Hebrews*. Fort Bragg, NC: Lost Coast, 2009.
Kierkegaard, Søren. *Fear and Trembling/Repetition*. Kierkegaard's Writings 6. Princeton: Princeton University Press, 1983.
King, Martin Luther, Jr. "I've Been to the Mountaintop." In *A Call to Conscience: The Landmark Speeches of Dr. Martin Luther King, Jr.*, edited by Clayborne Carson and Kris Shepard, 201–23. New York: Grand Central, 2002.
Kugel, James L. *The Great Shift: Encountering God in the Biblical Era*. Boston: Houghton Mifflin Harcourt, 2017.
Lanard, Noah. "The Dangerous History Behind Netanyahu's Amalek Rhetoric." *Mother Jones*, Nov. 3 2023. https://www.motherjones.com/politics/2023/11/benjamin-netanyahu-amalek-israel-palestine-gaza-saul-samuel-old-testament/.
Levenson, Jon. *Sinai and Zion: An Entry into the Jewish Bible*. San Francisco: HarperSanFrancisco, 1985.
Lewis, C. S. *Perelandra*. 1943. Reprint, New York: Scribner, 2003.
Lorde, Audre. *The Master's Tools Will Never Dismantle the Master's House*. London: Penguin, 2018.
McDowell, Catherine L. *The Image of God in the Garden of Eden The Creation of Humankind in Genesis 2:5—3:24 in Light of the Mīs Pî, Pīt Pî, and Wpt-r Rituals of Mesopotamia and Ancient Egypt*. Winona Lake, IN: Eisenbrauns, 2015.
Melville, Herman. *Moby-Dick*. 1851. Reprint, New York: Dover, 2003.
Morales, L. Michael. *The Tabernacle Pre-figured: Cosmic Mountain Ideology in Genesis and Exodus*. Leuven: Peeters, 2012.
Morrison, Toni. *Beloved*. London: Vintage, 2004.
Nietzsche, Friedrich. *The Gay Science: With a Prelude in Rhymes and an Appendix of Songs*. Translated by Walter Kaufmann. London: Vintage, 1974.
———. *The Portable Nietzsche*. Translated by Walter Kaufman. London: Penguin, 1977.
Oliver, Michael. *The Politics of Disablement: A Sociological Approach*. London: Palgrave Macmillan, 1990.
Otto, Rudolf. *The Idea of the Holy*. 1923. Reprint, Oxford: Oxford University Press, 1958.

Bibliography

Park, Andrew Sung. *Triune Atonement: Christ's Healing for Sinners, Victims, and the Whole Creation*. Louisville: Westminster John Knox, 2009.

Potok, Chaim. *My Name is Asher Lev*. New York: Anchor, 2003.

Powell, Mark Allen. *Loving Jesus*. Minneapolis: Fortress, 2004.

Powell, Marvin A. "Weights and Measures." *ABD* 6:897–908.

Prachett, Terry. *Small Gods*. New York: Harper, 2013.

Raheb, Mitri. *Decolonizing Palestine: The Land, the People, the Bible*. New York: Orbis, 2023.

Roggio, Sharon, dir. *1946: The Mistranslation That Shifted Culture*. United States: ACOWSAY, Quest for Biblical Truth, Sweetbreadstudios, and ZUM Communications, 2022.

Rollins, Peter. *The Divine Magician: The Disappearance of Religion and the Discovery of Faith*. New York: Howard, 2015.

Rubenstein, Richard. *After Auschwitz: Radical Theology and Contemporary Judaism*. Indianapolis: Bobbs-Merrill, 1966.

Smith, Mark S. *The Early History of God: YHWH and the Other Deities in Ancient Israel*. 2nd ed. Grand Rapids: Eerdmans, 2002.

Song, Angeline M. G. *A Postcolonial Woman's Encounter with Moses and Miriam*. New York: Palgrave Macmillan, 2015.

Steinbeck, John. *East of Eden*. 1952. Reprint, London: Penguin, 2002.

Stewart, Robert B., ed. *The Resurrection of Jesus: John Dominic Crossan and N. T. Wright in Dialogue*. Minneapolis: Fortress, 2005.

Wenham, Gordon J. "Sanctuary Symbolism in the Garden of Eden Story." *Proceedings of the World Congress of Jewish Studies* 9 (1986) 19–25.

Williams, Delores. *Sisters in the Wilderness: The Challenge of Womanist God-Talk*. New York: Orbis, 1993.

Wright, N. T. *Surprised by Hope: Rethinking Heaven, the Resurrection, and the Mission of the Church*. San Francisco: HarperOne, 2008.

Ancient Documents Index

HEBREW BIBLE
Genesis

Reference	Pages
1–3	111
1–2	9, 111
1:1—2:4	2–4, 5n5, 8–10, 108
1:2	7, 21, 92
1:6	8
1:9	39
1:11	8
1:16	4
1:20–21	4
1:20	8
1:22	8
1:24	8, 20
1:26	4, 11
1:27	3n4, 4
1:28	8
2	6–7, 9–10, 111
2:4–25	4–6
2:4b-5	7
2:5	5
2:7	92
2:9	6
2:15	9
2:16–17	11
3	11
3:4	11
3:6	29
3:22	9
4–11	112
4:1—6:7	12–13
4:2	13
4:23–24	13
5:24	17
6–9	20–22
6–7	21
6	17
6:1–4	71–72n2
6:1–2	13–16
6:4–18	
6:5–6	13
8:1–5	21–22
8:21	22
9:11	22
9:22	22
11:1–26	22–23
11:3	36
11:4	22
12–22	114
12:1–3	114
12:1	25
12:2–3	26
12:3	40, 97, 100, 108
14	19
15	27–29
15:12	27
15:1–3	27
15:5	27
15:6	97
15:8	27
15:9	27
16	29–30
16:3	29
17:18–21	30
18:16–33	31
22:1–19	25, 30–32
22:2	25

Genesis (continued)

22:13	31
22:18	41
37–50	34–35
50:19	35

Exodus

1–14	35–39
1–5	116
1:9–10	35
1:13–14	35–36
1:19	36
3:5	37, 117
3:7	38
5:7–8	36
12–14	116
15:1–12	116
19–24	xii
19–20	116
19	39–40
19:6	41, 51
19:12	117
20:4	6
24–26	116
24	41–42
24:1	41
24:10	41
32:9–14	37
34:6	37
40	42–43, 116

Leviticus

10	33–34
10:1	33
10:3	34
11:10	42
19:31	88n1
22:9	9

Numbers

1:31–33	88
13	19, 46–47
13:27	46
21:21–35	19

Deuteronomy

1:30	51
2–3	19
3:1–11	19
4:19	16
7:1–2, 5–6	49
17:14–20	54, 118, 119
17:16–17	54
18:10	88n1
21:23	84
22:11	42
32	112
32:7–9	15–16

Joshua

12:4–5	19
15	19

1 Samuel

8	51–52, 118, 119
8:20	51, 100
13:5	51
13:14	52, 119
15–16	51–52, 118
15:2–3	50
17	19
18:7	52
28	88n1

2 Samuel

7	45–46, 52–53, 118
7:3	45
7:5–7	46
7:7	52
11	54, 118
13:18	34

1 Kings

8	118
8:1–13	53
8:5	53
8:10–11	53
11–12	54, 118, 119

Ancient Documents Index

12:10–11	54
18	120
18:1–42	120
18:16–42	61–63
18:27	62
18:36–37	62
19:1–18	56–57, 120
19:4	57
21:1–16	15
22:19–21	15
22:22	15

2 Kings

11	6n7
11:18	6
24–25	120
25:1–21	64–65

2 Chronicles

22:10—23:21	6n7

Ezra

3	68–69, 84, 122
3:10–13	122
3:11–13	68

Job

1:6–7	15
38	4

Psalm

2:7	74
8	4, 110
16:10	88
22:1–2, 14–20	123–24
49:14	88
51:10–19	114
68:15–16	20
82	112
82:1–4	16
82:1	14
82:6–7	16
84:1–7	118
88:12	88
88:4–5	88
89:5–7	14
104	4
110	121–22
137:1–6	120
137:1–3	65
137:4	9
137:8–9	65–66

Proverbs

8	4

Ecclesiastes

9:5	88

Isaiah

2:1–5	127, 128
2:2–4	100–101
2:3	109
2:4	77
5:1–7	78
10:2	35
11:6	100
11:9	vi
14:4	13
14:12–14	14
63	106

Jeremiah

3:16	108
7:9–11	80
12:10	78

Ezekiel

10	65, 120
17:2–10	78
19:10–14	78
28	14
28:13–14	10
37:7–8	88
37:9–10	92
37:11–14	89

Daniel

4	17
12:2	89

Joel

2:28–32	125–126

Amos

5	120
5:18–20	63–64
5:21–24	60–61, 120
7	61

Jonah

1–4	58–59
4:2	59

Micah

4	127
4:1–2	100

Habakkuk

2:18–19	6

Zechariah

7:4	60

Malachi

4:5	63

PSEUDEPIGRAPHA

1 Enoch

1–9	112
6:5	19
10	19
12:4	19
15:7–9	19

Jubilees

10:1	71–72n2
10:5	71–72n2
10:8	71–72n2

NEW TESTAMENT

Matthew

6:10	84
17:1–13	67, 73–75
17:2	67
17:4	67, 75
18:20	92
23:31	63
23:37	63, 81
24:36	109
26:6–13	91
26:11	91
28:20	91

Mark

1–10	122
1:14	122
1:15	69
1:21–28	71–72
1:24	72
1:34	72
1:40–45	72
2:1–12	70–71
2:5–7	123
2:5	70
2:7	70
2:10	70
2:11	70
4:11	72
8:27–29	72–73
8:29	73, 84
9:2–13	67, 73–75
9:3	123
9:5	123
9:7	74
11:1—16:8	124
11:1–11	77, 124
11:10	77
11:12–25	78–81

11:13	78	1:8	98
11:14	78	1:9	126
11:16	79	2:1–13	92–94
11:17	78, 79	2:2	92
12:18–27	89	2:3	93
12:27	20	2:6	126
13	102	10	94–95, 126
14:32–52	81	10:13–15	94
14:53–65	81–82	15	126
14:61	81	15:1–21	95–96
14:65	82	15:1	95
14:66–72	95n6	15:9	96
15:1–15	82–83	15:19	96
15:2	82	17:28	10
15:9	83		
15:16–41	83–86		
15:26	84		

Romans

8:26	93n5
11:17	97
13:1–7	101

15:34	84, 124		
15:37	125		
15:39	85		
16	89–90		
16:8	90, 125		
16:9–11	90		
16:12–20	90		

1 Corinthians

12:10	93n5
13:1	93n5
14:2	93n5
14:18	93n5
15	126
15:20	89

Luke

9:28–36	67, 73–75
9:31	74
17:21	93
22:19	92
24	126
24:13–35	87–88
24:27	87

Galatians

1–4	96–98, 126
2:16	97
3:6	97
4:5	97

John

1	4
4:20	55
12:20–36	81
20:22	92
21:15–19	95n6

Ephesians

6:7	30

Philippians

2:6–7	11
2:6–8	84–85

Acts

1–2	126
1:1–11	8–87
1:6–8	87

1 Thessalonians

4:13—5:11	101

1 Timothy

6:1	30

Titus

2:9	30

Hebrews

8:5	49
11:19	31
12:18–19	xii
12:22–23	xii

1 Peter

3:18–20	71–72n2
3:19–20	19

Revelation

1–3	103
1:10	102
1:13–16	103
4–5	103–104
4:8	104
5:3	104
6:15–17	105
6–19	104–106
18–22	127
18:2–3	105
19–22	106–109
19	128
20:6	107
20:14	106, 107
21:1	107
21:3–4	127
21:22	128
21:25	108
22:1–3a	108

RABBINIC WRITINGS

b. Shabbat

119b	8n9

B'reishit Rabbah

3.9	8,n9
38.13	26n2

GRECO-ROMAN WRITINGS

Iliad

1.590	1n2

Odyssey

6.43–47	1n1

ISLAMIC WRITINGS

Qur'an

19.54	30
21.51–70	26, note 2

Hadith

4.583	30

www.ingramcontent.com/pod-product-compliance
Lightning Source LLC
Chambersburg PA
CBHW031458160426
43195CB00010BB/1020